50 Chinese Ramen Recipes for Home

By: Kelly Johnson

Table of Contents

- Classic Pork Ramen
- Spicy Sichuan Ramen
- Beef Noodle Soup
- Shrimp Ramen
- Vegetarian Ramen
- Garlic Sesame Ramen
- Five-Spice Duck Ramen
- Spicy Chicken Ramen
- Shanghai-Style Ramen
- Ginger Pork Ramen
- Tom Yum Ramen
- Taiwanese Beef Noodle Soup
- Braised Pork Belly Ramen
- Ma Po Tofu Ramen
- Mushroom Ramen
- Seafood Ramen
- Dan Dan Noodle Soup
- Beef Brisket Ramen
- Wonton Noodle Soup
- Chicken and Corn Ramen
- Hot and Sour Ramen
- Pork and Kimchi Ramen
- Beef Dumpling Ramen
- Spicy Peanut Ramen
- Vegetable Tofu Ramen
- Scallion Beef Ramen
- Sichuan Dan Dan Noodles
- Char Siu Ramen
- Chicken and Mushroom Ramen
- Braised Chicken Ramen
- Spicy Garlic Ramen
- Spicy Sesame Ramen
- Pork Rib Ramen
- Spinach and Egg Ramen
- Beef Shank Ramen

- XO Sauce Seafood Ramen
- Cumin Lamb Ramen
- Pickled Vegetables Ramen
- Pork and Cabbage Ramen
- Soy Sauce Chicken Ramen
- Fish Ball Noodle Soup
- Chili Oil Ramen
- Braised Beef Shank Ramen
- Egg Drop Ramen
- Ginger Scallion Ramen
- Spicy Pork and Bean Sprouts Ramen
- Chicken and Spinach Ramen
- Fried Tofu Ramen
- Sesame Peanut Ramen
- Double Cooked Pork Ramen

Classic Pork Ramen

Ingredients:

- 4 packs of fresh ramen noodles (or dried, follow package instructions)
- 4 cups chicken broth
- 2 cups water
- 1 tablespoon soy sauce
- 1 tablespoon mirin (Japanese sweet rice wine)
- 1 tablespoon sake (Japanese rice wine) or dry sherry
- 1 teaspoon sesame oil
- 1 teaspoon sugar
- Salt and white pepper to taste

For the pork:

- 1 lb pork belly or pork shoulder, thinly sliced
- 1 tablespoon soy sauce
- 1 tablespoon sake or dry sherry
- 1 teaspoon sugar
- Salt and pepper to taste

For toppings:

- 4 soft-boiled eggs, halved
- 2-3 green onions, thinly sliced
- 2 sheets nori (seaweed), cut into strips
- Bamboo shoots (menma), optional
- Corn kernels, optional
- Black garlic oil (mayu), optional

Instructions:

1. **Prepare the pork:** In a bowl, combine the pork slices with soy sauce, sake or sherry, sugar, salt, and pepper. Mix well and let marinate for at least 15-20 minutes.
2. **Cook the pork:** Heat a pan over medium-high heat. Add a little oil and cook the pork slices until browned and cooked through, about 2-3 minutes per side. Remove from heat and set aside.
3. **Prepare the broth:** In a large pot, combine chicken broth, water, soy sauce, mirin, sake or sherry, sesame oil, and sugar. Bring to a simmer over medium heat. Taste and adjust seasoning with salt and white pepper if needed.
4. **Cook the noodles:** Cook the ramen noodles according to package instructions. Drain and rinse under cold water to stop cooking. Divide noodles among serving bowls.
5. **Assemble the ramen:** Ladle the hot broth over the noodles in each bowl. Arrange slices of cooked pork, soft-boiled eggs, green onions, nori strips, bamboo shoots (if using), and any other toppings you prefer.

6. **Serve:** Optionally, drizzle with black garlic oil (mayu) for extra flavor. Serve immediately and enjoy your classic pork ramen!

This recipe serves 4. Adjust quantities based on your preference and enjoy your homemade classic pork ramen!

Spicy Sichuan Ramen

Ingredients:

- 4 packs of fresh ramen noodles (or dried, follow package instructions)
- 6 cups chicken broth
- 2 tablespoons Sichuan chili bean paste (Doubanjiang)
- 2 tablespoons soy sauce
- 1 tablespoon chili oil (adjust to taste)
- 1 tablespoon sesame oil
- 1 tablespoon rice vinegar
- 1 tablespoon sugar
- Salt to taste
- White pepper to taste

For the toppings:

- 1 lb boneless chicken thighs or breasts, thinly sliced
- 1 tablespoon soy sauce
- 1 tablespoon Shaoxing wine or dry sherry
- 1 teaspoon cornstarch
- 2 tablespoons vegetable oil
- 4 cloves garlic, minced
- 1-inch piece of ginger, minced
- 2 green onions, chopped
- 1 cup shiitake mushrooms, sliced
- 1 cup baby bok choy, chopped
- Soft-boiled eggs (optional)
- Bamboo shoots (menma, optional)
- Sesame seeds (for garnish, optional)
- Fresh cilantro (for garnish, optional)

Instructions:

1. **Marinate the chicken:** In a bowl, combine the sliced chicken with soy sauce, Shaoxing wine or sherry, and cornstarch. Mix well and let it marinate for 15-20 minutes.
2. **Prepare the broth:** In a large pot, combine chicken broth, Sichuan chili bean paste (Doubanjiang), soy sauce, chili oil, sesame oil, rice vinegar, and sugar. Bring to a simmer over medium heat. Taste and adjust seasoning with salt and white pepper if needed.
3. **Cook the noodles:** Cook the ramen noodles according to package instructions. Drain and rinse under cold water to stop cooking. Divide noodles among serving bowls.
4. **Cook the chicken and vegetables:** Heat vegetable oil in a skillet over medium-high heat. Add minced garlic and ginger, stir-fry for about 30 seconds until fragrant. Add marinated chicken slices and cook until browned and cooked through, about 3-4

minutes. Add green onions, shiitake mushrooms, and baby bok choy. Stir-fry for another 2-3 minutes until vegetables are tender.
5. **Assemble the ramen:** Ladle the hot broth over the noodles in each bowl. Top with the cooked chicken and vegetable mixture.
6. **Add toppings:** Optionally, add soft-boiled eggs, bamboo shoots (menma), sesame seeds, and fresh cilantro as desired.
7. **Serve:** Serve immediately and enjoy your spicy Sichuan ramen!

This recipe serves 4. Adjust quantities based on your preference and enjoy the spicy, flavorful goodness of homemade Sichuan ramen!

Beef Noodle Soup

Ingredients:

- 1 lb beef brisket or stewing beef, thinly sliced
- 8 cups beef broth (homemade or store-bought)
- 2 cups water
- 4 slices ginger
- 4 cloves garlic, crushed
- 2 star anise
- 2 cinnamon sticks
- 2 tablespoons soy sauce
- 1 tablespoon dark soy sauce (for color)
- 1 tablespoon Shaoxing wine or dry sherry
- 1 tablespoon rock sugar or regular sugar
- Salt and pepper to taste
- 1 lb fresh or dried Chinese wheat noodles (or any noodles of your choice)
- 4 baby bok choy, halved
- 4 green onions, chopped
- Fresh cilantro, chopped (for garnish)
- Red chili flakes or chili oil (optional, for heat)

Instructions:

1. **Prepare the beef:** If using brisket, blanch it in boiling water for a few minutes to remove impurities. Drain and rinse under cold water. Cut into thin slices. If using stewing beef, ensure it's thinly sliced.
2. **Make the broth:** In a large pot, combine beef broth, water, ginger slices, crushed garlic, star anise, cinnamon sticks, soy sauce, dark soy sauce, Shaoxing wine or sherry, and rock sugar or regular sugar. Bring to a boil over high heat, then reduce heat to low. Simmer for about 1 hour, partially covered, until the flavors meld together.
3. **Cook the noodles:** While the broth simmers, cook the noodles according to package instructions. Drain and rinse under cold water to stop cooking. Divide noodles among serving bowls.
4. **Prepare the vegetables:** Blanch the baby bok choy in boiling water for about 1-2 minutes until tender-crisp. Remove and set aside.
5. **Cook the beef:** Add the sliced beef to the simmering broth. Cook for about 5-7 minutes until the beef is cooked through and tender. Season with salt and pepper to taste.
6. **Assemble the soup:** Ladle the hot broth and beef over the noodles in each bowl. Add a few pieces of blanched baby bok choy. Top with chopped green onions, fresh cilantro, and red chili flakes or chili oil if desired.
7. **Serve:** Serve hot and enjoy your comforting Beef Noodle Soup!

This recipe serves 4. Adjust quantities based on your preference and enjoy this delicious and satisfying bowl of beef noodle soup!

Shrimp Ramen

Ingredients:

- 1 lb shrimp, peeled and deveined
- 4 packs of fresh ramen noodles (or dried, follow package instructions)
- 6 cups seafood or chicken broth
- 2 cups water
- 2 tablespoons soy sauce
- 1 tablespoon mirin (Japanese sweet rice wine)
- 1 tablespoon sesame oil
- 1 tablespoon miso paste (optional, for extra flavor)
- 1 teaspoon grated ginger
- 2 cloves garlic, minced
- 1 tablespoon vegetable oil
- Salt and pepper to taste
- Green onions, thinly sliced (for garnish)
- Nori (seaweed sheets), cut into strips (for garnish)
- Soft-boiled eggs, halved (optional, for topping)
- Bamboo shoots (menma, optional, for topping)
- Red chili flakes or chili oil (optional, for heat)

Instructions:

1. **Prepare the shrimp:** Heat vegetable oil in a large pot over medium-high heat. Add minced garlic and grated ginger, sauté for about 1 minute until fragrant. Add shrimp and cook until pink and cooked through, about 2-3 minutes. Remove shrimp from the pot and set aside.
2. **Make the broth:** In the same pot, add seafood or chicken broth, water, soy sauce, mirin, sesame oil, and miso paste (if using). Bring to a simmer over medium heat. Taste and adjust seasoning with salt and pepper if needed.
3. **Cook the noodles:** Cook the ramen noodles according to package instructions. Drain and rinse under cold water to stop cooking. Divide noodles among serving bowls.
4. **Assemble the ramen:** Ladle the hot broth over the noodles in each bowl. Arrange cooked shrimp on top.
5. **Add toppings:** Garnish with thinly sliced green onions, nori strips, and any additional toppings such as soft-boiled eggs and bamboo shoots (menma). Optionally, drizzle with red chili flakes or chili oil for extra heat.
6. **Serve:** Serve hot and enjoy your homemade Shrimp Ramen!

This recipe serves 4. Adjust quantities based on your preference and enjoy the delicious flavors of shrimp in this comforting bowl of ramen!

Vegetarian Ramen

Ingredients:

- 4 packs of fresh ramen noodles (or dried, follow package instructions)
- 6 cups vegetable broth
- 2 cups water
- 2 tablespoons soy sauce (or tamari for gluten-free option)
- 1 tablespoon miso paste
- 1 tablespoon sesame oil
- 1 tablespoon mirin (Japanese sweet rice wine) or rice vinegar
- 1 tablespoon grated ginger
- 2 cloves garlic, minced
- 1 tablespoon vegetable oil
- Salt and pepper to taste
- Tofu, cut into cubes or sliced (optional protein)
- Assorted vegetables such as:
    - 1 cup sliced shiitake mushrooms
    - 1 cup sliced bok choy or spinach
    - 1 cup sliced carrots
    - 1 cup sliced bamboo shoots (menma)
    - 1 cup sliced green onions
- Soft-boiled eggs (optional, for topping)
- Nori (seaweed sheets), cut into strips (optional, for garnish)
- Sesame seeds (optional, for garnish)
- Red chili flakes or chili oil (optional, for heat)

Instructions:

1. **Prepare the vegetables:** Heat vegetable oil in a large pot over medium-high heat. Add minced garlic and grated ginger, sauté for about 1 minute until fragrant. Add sliced mushrooms, carrots, and bamboo shoots (if using), and cook for about 3-4 minutes until slightly softened.
2. **Make the broth:** Add vegetable broth and water to the pot. Stir in soy sauce, miso paste, sesame oil, and mirin (or rice vinegar). Bring to a simmer over medium heat. Taste and adjust seasoning with salt and pepper if needed.
3. **Cook the noodles:** Cook the ramen noodles according to package instructions. Drain and rinse under cold water to stop cooking. Divide noodles among serving bowls.
4. **Add tofu (optional):** If using tofu, add tofu cubes to the simmering broth and cook for about 3-4 minutes until heated through.
5. **Assemble the ramen:** Ladle the hot broth and vegetables over the noodles in each bowl. Ensure each bowl has a good mix of vegetables.
6. **Add toppings:** Garnish with sliced green onions, nori strips, sesame seeds, and any additional toppings such as soft-boiled eggs and red chili flakes or chili oil if desired.
7. **Serve:** Serve hot and enjoy your comforting Vegetarian Ramen!

This recipe serves 4. Adjust quantities based on your preference and enjoy the wholesome flavors of this homemade Vegetarian Ramen!

Garlic Sesame Ramen

Ingredients:

- 4 packs of fresh ramen noodles (or dried, follow package instructions)
- 6 cups vegetable broth or chicken broth
- 2 cups water
- 4 cloves garlic, minced
- 2 tablespoons sesame oil
- 2 tablespoons soy sauce (or tamari for gluten-free option)
- 1 tablespoon mirin (Japanese sweet rice wine) or rice vinegar
- 1 tablespoon brown sugar (optional, for slight sweetness)
- 1 teaspoon grated ginger (optional)
- Salt and pepper to taste
- 1 tablespoon vegetable oil
- Thinly sliced green onions (for garnish)
- Sesame seeds (for garnish)
- Soft-boiled eggs (optional, for topping)
- Nori (seaweed sheets), cut into strips (optional, for garnish)
- Red chili flakes or chili oil (optional, for heat)

Instructions:

1. **Prepare the broth:** Heat vegetable oil in a large pot over medium heat. Add minced garlic and grated ginger (if using), sauté for about 1 minute until fragrant.
2. **Add liquids:** Add vegetable or chicken broth, water, sesame oil, soy sauce, mirin or rice vinegar, and brown sugar (if using). Stir well to combine. Bring to a simmer and let it simmer for about 10-15 minutes to allow the flavors to meld together. Taste and adjust seasoning with salt and pepper if needed.
3. **Cook the noodles:** Cook the ramen noodles according to package instructions. Drain and rinse under cold water to stop cooking. Divide noodles among serving bowls.
4. **Assemble the ramen:** Ladle the hot broth over the noodles in each bowl. Ensure each bowl has a good mix of garlic and sesame flavors.
5. **Add toppings:** Garnish with thinly sliced green onions, sesame seeds, and any additional toppings such as soft-boiled eggs, nori strips, and red chili flakes or chili oil if desired.
6. **Serve:** Serve hot and enjoy your aromatic Garlic Sesame Ramen!

This recipe serves 4. Adjust quantities based on your preference and enjoy the comforting and flavorful Garlic Sesame Ramen right at home!

Five-Spice Duck Ramen

Ingredients:

- 2 duck breasts
- 4 packs of fresh ramen noodles (or dried, follow package instructions)
- 6 cups chicken broth
- 2 cups water
- 2 tablespoons soy sauce
- 1 tablespoon mirin (Japanese sweet rice wine)
- 1 tablespoon sesame oil
- 1 tablespoon hoisin sauce
- 1 teaspoon five-spice powder
- 1 teaspoon grated ginger
- 2 cloves garlic, minced
- Salt and pepper to taste
- 1 tablespoon vegetable oil
- Green onions, thinly sliced (for garnish)
- Soft-boiled eggs (optional, for topping)
- Bamboo shoots (menma, optional, for topping)
- Nori (seaweed sheets), cut into strips (optional, for garnish)
- Red chili flakes or chili oil (optional, for heat)

Instructions:

1. **Prepare the duck:** Score the skin of the duck breasts in a criss-cross pattern (not cutting through to the meat). Season both sides with salt, pepper, and half of the five-spice powder.
2. **Cook the duck:** Heat vegetable oil in a skillet over medium-high heat. Add the duck breasts, skin side down, and cook for about 5-6 minutes until the skin is crispy and golden brown. Flip and cook for another 3-4 minutes for medium-rare, or until desired doneness. Remove from heat and let the duck rest for a few minutes before slicing thinly.
3. **Prepare the broth:** In a large pot, combine chicken broth, water, soy sauce, mirin, sesame oil, hoisin sauce, grated ginger, minced garlic, and the remaining half of the five-spice powder. Bring to a simmer over medium heat. Taste and adjust seasoning with salt and pepper if needed.
4. **Cook the noodles:** Cook the ramen noodles according to package instructions. Drain and rinse under cold water to stop cooking. Divide noodles among serving bowls.
5. **Assemble the ramen:** Ladle the hot broth over the noodles in each bowl. Arrange slices of the cooked duck on top.
6. **Add toppings:** Garnish with thinly sliced green onions, soft-boiled eggs (if using), bamboo shoots (menma), nori strips, and red chili flakes or chili oil if desired.
7. **Serve:** Serve hot and enjoy your flavorful Five-Spice Duck Ramen!

This recipe serves 4. Adjust quantities based on your preference and savor the delicious blend of duck and five-spice in this comforting bowl of ramen!

Spicy Chicken Ramen

Ingredients:

- 2 boneless, skinless chicken breasts, thinly sliced
- 4 packs of fresh ramen noodles (or dried, follow package instructions)
- 6 cups chicken broth
- 2 cups water
- 2 tablespoons soy sauce
- 1 tablespoon sesame oil
- 1 tablespoon chili garlic sauce or Sriracha (adjust to taste)
- 1 tablespoon miso paste
- 1 tablespoon rice vinegar
- 1 tablespoon brown sugar
- 1 teaspoon grated ginger
- 2 cloves garlic, minced
- Salt and pepper to taste
- 1 tablespoon vegetable oil
- Thinly sliced green onions (for garnish)
- Soft-boiled eggs (optional, for topping)
- Bamboo shoots (menma, optional, for topping)
- Nori (seaweed sheets), cut into strips (optional, for garnish)
- Red chili flakes or chili oil (optional, for extra heat)

Instructions:

1. **Prepare the chicken:** Season chicken breast slices with salt and pepper. Heat vegetable oil in a large pot over medium-high heat. Add chicken slices and cook until browned and cooked through, about 4-5 minutes per side. Remove chicken from pot and set aside.
2. **Make the broth:** In the same pot, add chicken broth, water, soy sauce, sesame oil, chili garlic sauce or Sriracha (adjust amount based on desired spiciness), miso paste, rice vinegar, brown sugar, grated ginger, and minced garlic. Stir well to combine. Bring to a simmer over medium heat. Taste and adjust seasoning with salt and pepper if needed.
3. **Cook the noodles:** Cook the ramen noodles according to package instructions. Drain and rinse under cold water to stop cooking. Divide noodles among serving bowls.
4. **Assemble the ramen:** Ladle the hot broth over the noodles in each bowl. Arrange slices of cooked chicken on top.
5. **Add toppings:** Garnish with thinly sliced green onions, soft-boiled eggs (if using), bamboo shoots (menma), nori strips, and red chili flakes or chili oil if desired.
6. **Serve:** Serve hot and enjoy your spicy and delicious Chicken Ramen!

This recipe serves 4. Adjust quantities based on your preference and spice tolerance, and enjoy this comforting bowl of Spicy Chicken Ramen at home!

Shanghai-Style Ramen

Ingredients:

- 4 packs of fresh ramen noodles (or dried, follow package instructions)
- 6 cups chicken or pork broth
- 2 cups water
- 1 tablespoon soy sauce
- 1 tablespoon oyster sauce
- 1 tablespoon Shaoxing wine (or dry sherry)
- 1 tablespoon sesame oil
- 1 tablespoon sugar
- 1 teaspoon grated ginger
- 2 cloves garlic, minced
- Salt and white pepper to taste
- 1 tablespoon vegetable oil
- Thinly sliced pork loin or pork belly (optional)
- Shanghai bok choy or baby bok choy, halved
- Green onions, thinly sliced (for garnish)
- Soft-boiled eggs (optional, for topping)
- Bamboo shoots (menma, optional, for topping)
- Red chili flakes or chili oil (optional, for heat)
- Sesame seeds (optional, for garnish)

Instructions:

1. **Prepare the broth:** Heat vegetable oil in a large pot over medium heat. Add minced garlic and grated ginger, sauté for about 1 minute until fragrant. Add chicken or pork broth, water, soy sauce, oyster sauce, Shaoxing wine, sesame oil, and sugar. Stir well to combine. Bring to a simmer over medium heat. Taste and adjust seasoning with salt and white pepper if needed.
2. **Cook the noodles:** Cook the ramen noodles according to package instructions. Drain and rinse under cold water to stop cooking. Divide noodles among serving bowls.
3. **Prepare the pork (if using):** Thinly slice pork loin or pork belly. Heat a skillet over medium-high heat and cook the pork slices until browned and cooked through, about 2-3 minutes per side. Remove from heat and set aside.
4. **Cook the bok choy:** Blanch Shanghai bok choy or baby bok choy in boiling water for about 1-2 minutes until tender-crisp. Remove and set aside.
5. **Assemble the ramen:** Ladle the hot broth over the noodles in each bowl. If using, arrange slices of cooked pork and blanched bok choy on top.
6. **Add toppings:** Garnish with thinly sliced green onions, soft-boiled eggs (if using), bamboo shoots (menma), red chili flakes or chili oil, and sesame seeds if desired.
7. **Serve:** Serve hot and enjoy your Shanghai-Style Ramen!

This recipe serves 4. Adjust quantities based on your preference and enjoy the comforting flavors of Shanghai-Style Ramen right at home!

Ginger Pork Ramen

Ingredients:

- 4 packs of fresh ramen noodles (or dried, follow package instructions)
- 6 cups chicken or pork broth
- 2 cups water
- 1 tablespoon soy sauce
- 1 tablespoon mirin (Japanese sweet rice wine)
- 1 tablespoon sesame oil
- 1 tablespoon grated ginger
- 2 cloves garlic, minced
- 1 tablespoon vegetable oil
- 1 lb pork loin or pork tenderloin, thinly sliced
- Salt and pepper to taste
- Thinly sliced green onions (for garnish)
- Soft-boiled eggs (optional, for topping)
- Bamboo shoots (menma, optional, for topping)
- Nori (seaweed sheets), cut into strips (optional, for garnish)
- Red chili flakes or chili oil (optional, for heat)
- Sesame seeds (optional, for garnish)

Instructions:

1. **Prepare the pork:** Heat vegetable oil in a large pot or skillet over medium-high heat. Add minced garlic and grated ginger, sauté for about 1 minute until fragrant. Add thinly sliced pork loin or pork tenderloin, season with salt and pepper, and cook until browned and cooked through, about 3-4 minutes per side. Remove from heat and set aside.
2. **Make the broth:** In the same pot or skillet (if using a separate pot for broth, transfer pork and aromatics), add chicken or pork broth, water, soy sauce, mirin, sesame oil, and any remaining ginger and garlic. Bring to a simmer over medium heat. Taste and adjust seasoning with salt and pepper if needed.
3. **Cook the noodles:** Cook the ramen noodles according to package instructions. Drain and rinse under cold water to stop cooking. Divide noodles among serving bowls.
4. **Assemble the ramen:** Ladle the hot broth over the noodles in each bowl. Arrange slices of cooked pork on top.
5. **Add toppings:** Garnish with thinly sliced green onions, soft-boiled eggs (if using), bamboo shoots (menma), nori strips, and red chili flakes or chili oil if desired. Sprinkle with sesame seeds for extra flavor.
6. **Serve:** Serve hot and enjoy your flavorful Ginger Pork Ramen!

This recipe serves 4. Adjust quantities based on your preference and enjoy the comforting and aromatic flavors of homemade Ginger Pork Ramen!

Tom Yum Ramen

Ingredients:

- 4 packs of fresh ramen noodles (or dried, follow package instructions)
- 6 cups chicken or vegetable broth
- 2 cups water
- 2 tablespoons Tom Yum paste or Tom Yum soup base
- 1 tablespoon fish sauce
- 1 tablespoon soy sauce
- 1 tablespoon lime juice
- 1 tablespoon brown sugar
- 1 tablespoon grated ginger
- 2 cloves garlic, minced
- 1 stalk lemongrass, bruised and cut into pieces
- 1-2 Thai chilies, sliced (adjust to taste)
- 1 cup sliced mushrooms (shiitake or button mushrooms)
- 1 cup cherry tomatoes, halved
- 1 cup baby bok choy or spinach leaves
- 1 tablespoon vegetable oil
- Salt and pepper to taste
- Fresh cilantro leaves, chopped (for garnish)
- Thinly sliced green onions (for garnish)
- Lime wedges (for serving)

Instructions:

1. **Prepare the broth:** Heat vegetable oil in a large pot over medium heat. Add minced garlic, grated ginger, lemongrass pieces, and Thai chilies. Sauté for about 1 minute until fragrant. Add Tom Yum paste or Tom Yum soup base and cook for another minute.
2. **Add liquids:** Pour in chicken or vegetable broth and water. Stir in fish sauce, soy sauce, lime juice, and brown sugar. Bring to a simmer over medium heat.
3. **Cook the noodles:** Add sliced mushrooms and cherry tomatoes to the simmering broth. Cook for about 3-4 minutes until mushrooms are tender.
4. **Prepare the noodles:** Cook the ramen noodles according to package instructions. Drain and rinse under cold water to stop cooking. Divide noodles among serving bowls.
5. **Add vegetables:** Add baby bok choy or spinach leaves to the simmering broth. Cook for another 1-2 minutes until wilted.
6. **Assemble the ramen:** Remove lemongrass pieces from the broth. Ladle the hot Tom Yum broth and vegetables over the noodles in each bowl.
7. **Add toppings:** Garnish with chopped cilantro leaves, thinly sliced green onions, and lime wedges for squeezing over the ramen.
8. **Serve:** Serve hot and enjoy your flavorful Tom Yum Ramen!

This recipe serves 4. Adjust quantities based on your preference and enjoy the spicy, sour, and aromatic flavors of Tom Yum combined with comforting ramen noodles!

Taiwanese Beef Noodle Soup

Ingredients:

- 1 lb beef shank or brisket, cut into chunks
- 4 packs of fresh ramen noodles (or dried, follow package instructions)
- 6 cups beef broth
- 2 cups water
- 1/4 cup soy sauce
- 2 tablespoons rice wine or Shaoxing wine
- 1 tablespoon rock sugar or regular sugar
- 4 slices ginger
- 4 cloves garlic, crushed
- 2 star anise
- 2 cinnamon sticks
- 1 teaspoon Sichuan peppercorns (optional, for a numbing effect)
- Salt and pepper to taste
- 1 tablespoon vegetable oil
- Green onions, chopped (for garnish)
- Bok choy or Shanghai bok choy, chopped (optional)
- Chili oil or chili paste (optional, for heat)

Instructions:

1. **Prepare the beef:** In a large pot, heat vegetable oil over medium-high heat. Add the beef chunks and sear until browned on all sides, about 3-4 minutes. Remove the beef from the pot and set aside.
2. **Make the broth:** In the same pot, add beef broth, water, soy sauce, rice wine, rock sugar or sugar, ginger slices, crushed garlic, star anise, cinnamon sticks, and Sichuan peppercorns (if using). Bring to a boil over high heat.
3. **Simmer the broth:** Once boiling, reduce heat to low and let the broth simmer. Skim off any foam that rises to the surface. Cover and simmer for about 1.5 to 2 hours, or until the beef is tender and falls apart easily. Alternatively, you can cook it in a pressure cooker for 30-40 minutes.
4. **Cook the noodles:** While the broth simmers, cook the ramen noodles according to package instructions. Drain and rinse under cold water to stop cooking. Divide noodles among serving bowls.
5. **Prepare the vegetables (optional):** Blanch chopped bok choy or Shanghai bok choy in boiling water for about 1-2 minutes until tender-crisp. Remove and set aside.
6. **Serve the soup:** Once the beef is tender, remove it from the broth and slice or shred it. Discard the ginger slices, garlic, star anise, and cinnamon sticks from the broth. Taste the broth and adjust seasoning with salt and pepper if needed.
7. **Assemble the soup:** Ladle the hot broth over the noodles in each bowl. Add slices or shredded beef on top. Optionally, add blanched bok choy or Shanghai bok choy.

8. **Garnish and serve:** Garnish with chopped green onions and optionally drizzle with chili oil or add chili paste for extra heat.
9. **Serve hot:** Serve immediately and enjoy your homemade Taiwanese Beef Noodle Soup!

This recipe serves 4. Adjust quantities based on your preference and savor the rich and comforting flavors of this Taiwanese classic.

Braised Pork Belly Ramen

Ingredients:

For the Braised Pork Belly:

- 1 lb pork belly, skin removed and cut into thick slices
- 2 cups water
- 1/2 cup soy sauce
- 1/4 cup mirin (Japanese sweet rice wine)
- 1/4 cup sake or dry sherry
- 1/4 cup brown sugar
- 4 cloves garlic, crushed
- 2 slices ginger
- 2 green onions, cut into 2-inch pieces
- 1 star anise (optional)
- 1 cinnamon stick (optional)

For the Ramen:

- 4 packs of fresh ramen noodles (or dried, follow package instructions)
- 6 cups pork or chicken broth
- 2 cups water
- 2 tablespoons soy sauce
- 1 tablespoon miso paste (optional, for extra flavor)
- 1 tablespoon sesame oil
- 1 tablespoon grated ginger
- 2 cloves garlic, minced
- Salt and pepper to taste
- 1 tablespoon vegetable oil
- Soft-boiled eggs, halved (optional, for topping)
- Bamboo shoots (menma, optional, for topping)
- Nori (seaweed sheets), cut into strips (optional, for garnish)
- Thinly sliced green onions (for garnish)
- Red chili flakes or chili oil (optional, for heat)

Instructions:

For the Braised Pork Belly:

1. In a large pot, combine water, soy sauce, mirin, sake or dry sherry, brown sugar, crushed garlic, ginger slices, green onions, star anise (if using), and cinnamon stick (if using). Bring to a boil over high heat.
2. Add the pork belly slices to the pot, ensuring they are submerged in the liquid. Reduce heat to low, cover, and simmer for about 1.5 to 2 hours, or until the pork belly is tender and can be easily pierced with a fork.

3. Remove the pork belly from the pot and set aside. Strain and reserve the braising liquid. Discard the solids.

For the Ramen:

1. Heat vegetable oil in a large pot over medium heat. Add minced garlic and grated ginger, sauté for about 1 minute until fragrant.
2. Pour in pork or chicken broth and water. Stir in soy sauce, miso paste (if using), sesame oil, and the reserved braising liquid from the pork belly. Bring to a simmer over medium heat. Taste and adjust seasoning with salt and pepper if needed.
3. Cook the ramen noodles according to package instructions. Drain and rinse under cold water to stop cooking. Divide noodles among serving bowls.
4. Slice the braised pork belly into thin slices or chunks.
5. Assemble the ramen bowls by ladling the hot broth over the noodles. Arrange slices of braised pork belly on top.
6. Add optional toppings such as soft-boiled eggs, bamboo shoots (menma), nori strips, thinly sliced green onions, and red chili flakes or chili oil for extra heat.
7. Serve hot and enjoy your delicious Braised Pork Belly Ramen!

This recipe serves 4. Adjust quantities based on your preference and enjoy the rich and savory flavors of this indulgent ramen dish!

Ma Po Tofu Ramen

Ingredients:

- 4 packs of fresh ramen noodles (or dried, follow package instructions)
- 1 block (about 14 oz) firm tofu, cut into cubes
- 1 tablespoon vegetable oil
- 2 cloves garlic, minced
- 1 tablespoon grated ginger
- 2 green onions, chopped (white and green parts separated)
- 1/4 lb ground pork (optional)
- 2 tablespoons doubanjiang (Chinese fermented chili bean paste)
- 1 tablespoon soy sauce
- 1 tablespoon hoisin sauce
- 1 tablespoon Shaoxing wine (or dry sherry)
- 2 cups chicken or vegetable broth
- 1 cup water
- 1 teaspoon Sichuan peppercorns, toasted and ground
- 1 teaspoon chili oil (adjust to taste)
- 1 teaspoon sesame oil
- 1 tablespoon cornstarch mixed with 2 tablespoons water (optional, for thickening)
- Salt and pepper to taste
- Thinly sliced green onions and cilantro (for garnish)
- Soft-boiled eggs (optional, for topping)
- Nori (seaweed sheets), cut into strips (optional, for garnish)

Instructions:

1. **Prepare the tofu:** Pat dry the tofu cubes with paper towels. Heat vegetable oil in a large pot or deep skillet over medium-high heat. Add tofu cubes and fry until golden brown on all sides, about 5-7 minutes. Remove tofu from pot and set aside.
2. **Make the base:** In the same pot, add minced garlic, grated ginger, and the white parts of the chopped green onions. Sauté for about 1 minute until fragrant. If using ground pork, add it to the pot and cook until browned and cooked through.
3. **Add flavoring ingredients:** Stir in doubanjiang (Chinese fermented chili bean paste), soy sauce, hoisin sauce, and Shaoxing wine. Cook for another minute to combine flavors.
4. **Add liquids:** Pour in chicken or vegetable broth and water. Bring to a simmer over medium heat.
5. **Season and simmer:** Add ground Sichuan peppercorns, chili oil, and sesame oil. Taste and adjust seasoning with salt and pepper as needed. If you prefer a thicker sauce, stir in the cornstarch mixture and simmer until slightly thickened.
6. **Cook the noodles:** Cook the ramen noodles according to package instructions. Drain and rinse under cold water to stop cooking. Divide noodles among serving bowls.

7. **Assemble the ramen bowls:** Ladle the hot Ma Po Tofu mixture over the noodles in each bowl. Arrange fried tofu cubes on top.
8. **Add toppings:** Garnish with thinly sliced green onions (green parts), cilantro, soft-boiled eggs (if using), and nori strips.
9. **Serve hot:** Serve immediately and enjoy your flavorful Ma Po Tofu Ramen!

This recipe serves 4. Adjust quantities based on your preference and enjoy the bold and spicy flavors of this fusion ramen dish!

Mushroom Ramen

Ingredients:

- 4 packs of fresh ramen noodles (or dried, follow package instructions)
- 6 cups vegetable or mushroom broth
- 2 cups water
- 1 tablespoon soy sauce (or tamari for gluten-free)
- 1 tablespoon miso paste
- 1 tablespoon sesame oil
- 1 tablespoon mirin (Japanese sweet rice wine)
- 1 tablespoon grated ginger
- 2 cloves garlic, minced
- 1 tablespoon vegetable oil
- 1 lb mixed mushrooms (such as shiitake, cremini, and oyster), sliced
- Salt and pepper to taste
- Thinly sliced green onions (for garnish)
- Soft-boiled eggs (optional, for topping)
- Bamboo shoots (menma, optional, for topping)
- Nori (seaweed sheets), cut into strips (optional, for garnish)
- Red chili flakes or chili oil (optional, for heat)

Instructions:

1. **Prepare the mushrooms:** Heat vegetable oil in a large pot over medium-high heat. Add sliced mushrooms and cook until they release their moisture and start to brown, about 5-7 minutes.
2. **Make the broth:** Add minced garlic and grated ginger to the pot with the mushrooms. Sauté for 1-2 minutes until fragrant. Pour in vegetable or mushroom broth and water.
3. **Flavor the broth:** Stir in soy sauce, miso paste, sesame oil, and mirin. Bring to a simmer over medium heat. Taste and adjust seasoning with salt and pepper if needed.
4. **Cook the noodles:** Cook the ramen noodles according to package instructions. Drain and rinse under cold water to stop cooking. Divide noodles among serving bowls.
5. **Assemble the ramen bowls:** Ladle the hot mushroom broth over the noodles in each bowl.
6. **Add toppings:** Garnish with thinly sliced green onions, soft-boiled eggs (if using), bamboo shoots (menma), nori strips, and red chili flakes or chili oil if desired.
7. **Serve hot:** Serve immediately and enjoy your comforting Mushroom Ramen!

This recipe serves 4. Adjust quantities based on your preference and enjoy the hearty and flavorful Mushroom Ramen, perfect for mushroom lovers!

Seafood Ramen

Ingredients:

- 4 packs of fresh ramen noodles (or dried, follow package instructions)
- 6 cups seafood broth (you can make this by simmering seafood shells, such as shrimp or crab, in water for about 30 minutes and straining)
- 2 cups water
- 1 tablespoon soy sauce (or tamari for gluten-free)
- 1 tablespoon miso paste
- 1 tablespoon sesame oil
- 1 tablespoon mirin (Japanese sweet rice wine)
- 1 tablespoon grated ginger
- 2 cloves garlic, minced
- 1 tablespoon vegetable oil
- 1/2 lb shrimp, peeled and deveined
- 1/2 lb scallops
- 1/2 lb mixed seafood (such as squid rings, mussels, or fish fillet)
- Salt and pepper to taste
- Thinly sliced green onions (for garnish)
- Soft-boiled eggs (optional, for topping)
- Nori (seaweed sheets), cut into strips (optional, for garnish)
- Red chili flakes or chili oil (optional, for heat)

Instructions:

1. **Prepare the seafood:** Heat vegetable oil in a large pot over medium-high heat. Add shrimp, scallops, and mixed seafood. Cook until seafood is just cooked through, about 3-4 minutes. Remove seafood from pot and set aside.
2. **Make the broth:** In the same pot, add minced garlic and grated ginger. Sauté for 1-2 minutes until fragrant. Pour in seafood broth and water.
3. **Flavor the broth:** Stir in soy sauce, miso paste, sesame oil, and mirin. Bring to a simmer over medium heat. Taste and adjust seasoning with salt and pepper if needed.
4. **Cook the noodles:** Cook the ramen noodles according to package instructions. Drain and rinse under cold water to stop cooking. Divide noodles among serving bowls.
5. **Assemble the ramen bowls:** Ladle the hot seafood broth over the noodles in each bowl.
6. **Add cooked seafood:** Arrange cooked shrimp, scallops, and mixed seafood on top of the ramen bowls.
7. **Add toppings:** Garnish with thinly sliced green onions, soft-boiled eggs (if using), nori strips, and red chili flakes or chili oil if desired.
8. **Serve hot:** Serve immediately and enjoy your flavorful Seafood Ramen!

This recipe serves 4. Adjust quantities based on your preference and enjoy the delicious flavors of seafood combined with comforting ramen noodles!

Dan Dan Noodle Soup

Ingredients:

For the Soup Base:

- 4 packs of fresh ramen noodles (or dried, follow package instructions)
- 6 cups chicken or vegetable broth
- 2 cups water
- 2 tablespoons soy sauce
- 1 tablespoon sesame oil
- 1 tablespoon rice vinegar
- 1 tablespoon brown sugar
- 1 tablespoon chili oil (adjust to taste)
- 1 tablespoon Sichuan peppercorns, toasted and ground
- Salt to taste

For the Ground Meat:

- 1/2 lb ground pork or chicken
- 2 cloves garlic, minced
- 1 tablespoon vegetable oil
- 1 tablespoon doubanjiang (Chinese chili bean paste)
- 1 tablespoon soy sauce
- 1 tablespoon Shaoxing wine (or dry sherry)
- 1 tablespoon brown sugar
- 1/2 cup water or chicken broth

For Garnish (optional):

- Thinly sliced green onions
- Chopped cilantro
- Crushed peanuts
- Thinly sliced cucumber

Instructions:

1. **Prepare the Soup Base:**
   - In a large pot, combine chicken or vegetable broth, water, soy sauce, sesame oil, rice vinegar, brown sugar, chili oil, and ground Sichuan peppercorns. Bring to a simmer over medium heat. Taste and adjust seasoning with salt if needed.
2. **Cook the Ground Meat:**
   - Heat vegetable oil in a skillet over medium-high heat. Add minced garlic and cook for about 30 seconds until fragrant.
   - Add ground pork or chicken to the skillet and cook until browned and cooked through.

- Stir in doubanjiang (Chinese chili bean paste), soy sauce, Shaoxing wine, and brown sugar. Cook for another minute.
- Pour in water or chicken broth and simmer for 5-7 minutes until the sauce thickens slightly. Set aside.

3. **Cook the Noodles:**
   - Cook the ramen noodles according to package instructions. Drain and rinse under cold water to stop cooking. Divide noodles among serving bowls.
4. **Assemble the Dan Dan Noodle Soup:**
   - Ladle the hot soup base over the noodles in each bowl.
   - Top each bowl with a generous spoonful of the cooked ground meat mixture.
5. **Garnish and Serve:**
   - Garnish with thinly sliced green onions, chopped cilantro, crushed peanuts, and thinly sliced cucumber if desired.
6. **Serve Immediately:**
   - Serve hot and enjoy your flavorful Dan Dan Noodle Soup!

This recipe serves 4. Adjust quantities based on your preference and enjoy the bold and spicy flavors of this classic Sichuan dish in soup form!

Beef Brisket Ramen

Ingredients:

- 1 lb beef brisket
- 4 packs of fresh ramen noodles (or dried, follow package instructions)
- 6 cups beef broth
- 2 cups water
- 1 onion, quartered
- 2 carrots, peeled and chopped into large chunks
- 2 stalks celery, chopped into large chunks
- 4 cloves garlic, smashed
- 1 piece ginger, about 2 inches, sliced
- 2 tablespoons soy sauce
- 1 tablespoon mirin (Japanese sweet rice wine)
- 1 tablespoon sesame oil
- Salt and pepper to taste
- Thinly sliced green onions (for garnish)
- Soft-boiled eggs (optional, for topping)
- Bamboo shoots (menma, optional, for topping)
- Nori (seaweed sheets), cut into strips (optional, for garnish)
- Red chili flakes or chili oil (optional, for heat)

Instructions:

1. **Prepare the Beef Brisket:**
    - Place the beef brisket in a large pot and add enough water to cover it. Bring to a boil over high heat and cook for about 5 minutes to remove any impurities. Drain and rinse the brisket under cold water.
2. **Cook the Brisket:**
    - Return the rinsed brisket to the pot. Add beef broth, water, quartered onion, chopped carrots, chopped celery, smashed garlic cloves, and sliced ginger.
    - Bring to a boil over high heat. Skim off any foam that rises to the surface. Reduce heat to low, cover, and simmer for about 2.5 to 3 hours, or until the brisket is tender and easily pierced with a fork.
3. **Prepare the Broth:**
    - Remove the brisket from the pot and set aside to cool slightly. Strain the broth through a fine mesh sieve into another pot. Discard the solids.
    - Stir in soy sauce, mirin, and sesame oil. Season with salt and pepper to taste. Keep the broth warm over low heat.
4. **Cook the Noodles:**
    - Cook the ramen noodles according to package instructions. Drain and rinse under cold water to stop cooking. Divide noodles among serving bowls.
5. **Assemble the Ramen Bowls:**
    - Slice the cooked beef brisket against the grain into thin slices.

- Ladle the hot broth over the noodles in each bowl.
- Arrange slices of beef brisket on top of each bowl of ramen.

6. **Add Toppings:**
    - Garnish with thinly sliced green onions, soft-boiled eggs (if using), bamboo shoots (menma), nori strips, and red chili flakes or chili oil if desired.
7. **Serve Immediately:**
    - Serve hot and enjoy your comforting Beef Brisket Ramen!

This recipe serves 4. Adjust quantities based on your preference and enjoy the rich flavors of tender beef brisket and savory broth in this satisfying ramen dish!

Wonton Noodle Soup

Ingredients:

For the Wontons:

- 1/2 lb ground pork or shrimp, or a combination of both
- 1 tablespoon soy sauce
- 1 tablespoon oyster sauce
- 1 tablespoon sesame oil
- 1 tablespoon Shaoxing wine (or dry sherry)
- 1 teaspoon sugar
- 1/2 teaspoon white pepper
- 1 teaspoon grated ginger
- 2 cloves garlic, minced
- 1 green onion, finely chopped
- Wonton wrappers (round or square)

For the Soup:

- 4 packs of fresh ramen noodles (or dried, follow package instructions)
- 6 cups chicken or pork broth
- 2 cups water
- 1 tablespoon soy sauce (or to taste)
- 1 tablespoon oyster sauce
- 1 tablespoon sesame oil
- 1 tablespoon Shaoxing wine (or dry sherry)
- Salt and white pepper to taste
- Thinly sliced green onions (for garnish)
- Bok choy or baby spinach (optional, blanched for serving)
- Thinly sliced fresh red chilies (optional, for garnish)

Instructions:

Making the Wontons:

1. In a mixing bowl, combine ground pork or shrimp with soy sauce, oyster sauce, sesame oil, Shaoxing wine, sugar, white pepper, grated ginger, minced garlic, and chopped green onion. Mix until well combined.
2. Place a small spoonful of the filling in the center of a wonton wrapper. Wet the edges of the wrapper with water, then fold in half to form a triangle or a pouch, pressing to seal the edges tightly. Repeat until all filling is used.
3. Bring a large pot of water to a boil. Cook the wontons in batches for about 5 minutes or until they float to the surface and are cooked through. Remove with a slotted spoon and set aside.

Making the Soup:

1. In a large pot, bring chicken or pork broth and water to a simmer over medium heat.
2. Stir in soy sauce, oyster sauce, sesame oil, and Shaoxing wine. Season with salt and white pepper to taste.
3. Cook the ramen noodles according to package instructions. Drain and rinse under cold water to stop cooking. Divide noodles among serving bowls.
4. Ladle the hot soup over the noodles in each bowl.
5. Add cooked wontons to each bowl of soup.
6. Garnish with thinly sliced green onions, blanched bok choy or baby spinach (if using), and sliced fresh red chilies (if desired).
7. Serve hot and enjoy your homemade Wonton Noodle Soup!

This recipe serves 4. Adjust quantities based on your preference and enjoy the comforting and savory flavors of this classic dish!

Chicken and Corn Ramen

Ingredients:

- 4 packs of fresh ramen noodles (or dried, follow package instructions)
- 2 boneless, skinless chicken breasts
- 6 cups chicken broth
- 2 cups water
- 1 cup sweet corn kernels (fresh or frozen)
- 1 carrot, thinly sliced
- 1 cup sliced shiitake mushrooms (optional)
- 2 cloves garlic, minced
- 1 tablespoon grated ginger
- 2 tablespoons soy sauce (or tamari for gluten-free)
- 1 tablespoon sesame oil
- Salt and pepper to taste
- Thinly sliced green onions (for garnish)
- Soft-boiled eggs (optional, for topping)
- Nori (seaweed sheets), cut into strips (optional, for garnish)
- Red chili flakes or chili oil (optional, for heat)

Instructions:

1. **Cook the Chicken:**
     - In a large pot, bring chicken broth and water to a boil. Add chicken breasts and cook for about 15-20 minutes, or until cooked through and no longer pink inside.
     - Remove chicken from the pot and shred using two forks. Set aside.
2. **Prepare the Broth:**
     - In the same pot with the chicken broth, add sweet corn kernels, sliced carrot, and sliced shiitake mushrooms (if using). Bring to a simmer over medium heat.
3. **Add Flavorings:**
     - Stir in minced garlic, grated ginger, soy sauce, and sesame oil. Season with salt and pepper to taste.
4. **Cook the Noodles:**
     - Cook the ramen noodles according to package instructions. Drain and rinse under cold water to stop cooking. Divide noodles among serving bowls.
5. **Assemble the Ramen Bowls:**
     - Ladle the hot broth and vegetables over the noodles in each bowl.
     - Top with shredded chicken.
6. **Add Toppings:**
     - Garnish with thinly sliced green onions, soft-boiled eggs (if using), nori strips, and red chili flakes or chili oil if desired.
7. **Serve Immediately:**
     - Serve hot and enjoy your comforting Chicken and Corn Ramen!

This recipe serves 4. Adjust quantities based on your preference and enjoy the wholesome and flavorful combination of chicken, corn, and noodles in this comforting ramen dish!

Hot and Sour Ramen

Ingredients:

- 4 packs of fresh ramen noodles (or dried, follow package instructions)
- 6 cups chicken or vegetable broth
- 2 cups water
- 1/4 cup rice vinegar
- 3 tablespoons soy sauce (or tamari for gluten-free)
- 1 tablespoon chili garlic sauce (adjust to taste)
- 1 tablespoon sesame oil
- 1 tablespoon grated ginger
- 2 cloves garlic, minced
- 1 tablespoon sugar
- 1 tablespoon cornstarch mixed with 2 tablespoons water
- 1 cup sliced shiitake mushrooms (fresh or rehydrated from dried)
- 1/2 cup bamboo shoots, sliced
- 1/2 cup firm tofu, diced
- 1 egg, beaten
- Salt and pepper to taste
- Thinly sliced green onions (for garnish)
- Thinly sliced fresh red chilies (for garnish, optional)
- Toasted sesame seeds (for garnish, optional)

Instructions:

1. **Prepare the Broth:**
   - In a large pot, combine chicken or vegetable broth, water, rice vinegar, soy sauce, chili garlic sauce, sesame oil, grated ginger, minced garlic, and sugar. Bring to a simmer over medium heat.
2. **Thicken the Broth:**
   - Stir in the cornstarch mixture, stirring constantly until the broth thickens slightly.
3. **Add Mushrooms, Bamboo Shoots, and Tofu:**
   - Add sliced shiitake mushrooms, bamboo shoots, and diced tofu to the broth. Simmer for about 5-7 minutes until mushrooms are tender and tofu is heated through.
4. **Prepare the Ramen Noodles:**
   - Cook the ramen noodles according to package instructions. Drain and rinse under cold water to stop cooking. Divide noodles among serving bowls.
5. **Finish the Soup:**
   - Slowly pour the beaten egg into the simmering broth while stirring gently to create egg ribbons.
6. **Season and Serve:**
   - Taste and adjust seasoning with salt and pepper if needed.
7. **Assemble the Ramen Bowls:**

- Ladle the hot and sour broth with vegetables over the noodles in each bowl.
8. **Garnish and Serve:**
   - Garnish with thinly sliced green onions, thinly sliced fresh red chilies (if using), and toasted sesame seeds if desired.
9. **Serve Immediately:**
   - Serve hot and enjoy your flavorful Hot and Sour Ramen!

This recipe serves 4. Adjust quantities based on your preference and enjoy the tangy, spicy, and comforting flavors of this Hot and Sour Ramen!

Pork and Kimchi Ramen

Ingredients:

- 4 packs of fresh ramen noodles (or dried, follow package instructions)
- 6 cups pork or chicken broth
- 2 cups water
- 1 cup kimchi, chopped
- 1/2 lb pork belly or pork shoulder, thinly sliced
- 2 tablespoons soy sauce
- 1 tablespoon sesame oil
- 1 tablespoon mirin (Japanese sweet rice wine)
- 1 tablespoon gochujang (Korean chili paste)
- 1 tablespoon grated ginger
- 2 cloves garlic, minced
- 1 tablespoon vegetable oil
- 2 green onions, chopped (white and green parts separated)
- Salt and pepper to taste
- Soft-boiled eggs (optional, for topping)
- Nori (seaweed sheets), cut into strips (optional, for garnish)
- Toasted sesame seeds (optional, for garnish)

Instructions:

1. **Prepare the Pork:**
   - Heat vegetable oil in a large pot or deep skillet over medium-high heat. Add sliced pork belly or pork shoulder and cook until browned and crispy. Remove from pot and set aside.
2. **Make the Broth:**
   - In the same pot, add minced garlic, grated ginger, and the white parts of the chopped green onions. Sauté for about 1 minute until fragrant.
   - Stir in soy sauce, sesame oil, mirin, and gochujang. Cook for another minute to combine flavors.
3. **Add Kimchi and Broth:**
   - Add chopped kimchi to the pot and cook for 2-3 minutes until heated through.
   - Pour in pork or chicken broth and water. Bring to a simmer over medium heat. Taste and adjust seasoning with salt and pepper if needed.
4. **Cook the Noodles:**
   - Cook the ramen noodles according to package instructions. Drain and rinse under cold water to stop cooking. Divide noodles among serving bowls.
5. **Assemble the Ramen Bowls:**
   - Ladle the hot broth with kimchi over the noodles in each bowl.
   - Top with the crispy pork slices.
6. **Add Toppings:**

- Garnish with the green parts of chopped green onions, soft-boiled eggs (if using), nori strips, and toasted sesame seeds if desired.
7. **Serve Immediately:**
   - Serve hot and enjoy your flavorful Pork and Kimchi Ramen!

This recipe serves 4. Adjust quantities based on your preference and enjoy the bold and savory flavors of pork and kimchi in this delicious ramen dish!

Beef Dumpling Ramen

Ingredients:

For the Beef Dumplings:

- 1/2 lb ground beef
- 1 tablespoon soy sauce
- 1 tablespoon oyster sauce
- 1 tablespoon sesame oil
- 1 tablespoon Shaoxing wine (or dry sherry)
- 1 teaspoon grated ginger
- 2 cloves garlic, minced
- 2 green onions, finely chopped
- Salt and pepper to taste
- Wonton wrappers (round or square)

For the Ramen:

- 4 packs of fresh ramen noodles (or dried, follow package instructions)
- 6 cups beef broth
- 2 cups water
- 1 tablespoon soy sauce (or to taste)
- 1 tablespoon sesame oil
- 1 tablespoon mirin (Japanese sweet rice wine)
- 1 tablespoon grated ginger
- 2 cloves garlic, minced
- Salt and pepper to taste
- Thinly sliced green onions (for garnish)
- Soft-boiled eggs (optional, for topping)
- Nori (seaweed sheets), cut into strips (optional, for garnish)
- Red chili flakes or chili oil (optional, for heat)

Instructions:

Making the Beef Dumplings:

1. In a mixing bowl, combine ground beef with soy sauce, oyster sauce, sesame oil, Shaoxing wine, grated ginger, minced garlic, chopped green onions, salt, and pepper.
2. Place a small spoonful of the filling in the center of a wonton wrapper. Wet the edges of the wrapper with water, then fold in half to form a triangle or a pouch, pressing to seal the edges tightly. Repeat until all filling is used.
3. Bring a large pot of water to a boil. Cook the dumplings in batches for about 5 minutes or until they float to the surface and are cooked through. Remove with a slotted spoon and set aside.

Making the Ramen:

1. In a large pot, combine beef broth and water. Bring to a simmer over medium heat.
2. Stir in soy sauce, sesame oil, mirin, grated ginger, minced garlic, salt, and pepper. Adjust seasoning to taste.
3. Cook the ramen noodles according to package instructions. Drain and rinse under cold water to stop cooking. Divide noodles among serving bowls.
4. Ladle the hot broth over the noodles in each bowl.
5. Arrange beef dumplings on top of each bowl of ramen.
6. Garnish with thinly sliced green onions, soft-boiled eggs (if using), nori strips, and red chili flakes or chili oil if desired.
7. Serve immediately and enjoy your Beef Dumpling Ramen!

This recipe serves 4. Adjust quantities based on your preference and enjoy the delicious combination of beef dumplings and ramen noodles in a savory broth!

Spicy Peanut Ramen

Ingredients:

- 4 packs of fresh ramen noodles (or dried, follow package instructions)
- 6 cups vegetable or chicken broth
- 2 cups water
- 1/2 cup smooth peanut butter
- 2 tablespoons soy sauce (or tamari for gluten-free)
- 1 tablespoon rice vinegar
- 1 tablespoon sesame oil
- 1 tablespoon honey or brown sugar
- 1-2 teaspoons sriracha sauce (adjust to taste)
- 2 cloves garlic, minced
- 1 tablespoon grated ginger
- 1 red bell pepper, thinly sliced
- 1 cup shredded cabbage or coleslaw mix
- 1/2 cup sliced scallions (green onions)
- Salt and pepper to taste
- Crushed peanuts (for garnish)
- Lime wedges (for serving)

Instructions:

1. **Prepare the Spicy Peanut Sauce:**
    - In a small bowl, whisk together peanut butter, soy sauce, rice vinegar, sesame oil, honey or brown sugar, sriracha sauce, minced garlic, and grated ginger until smooth. Set aside.
2. **Make the Broth:**
    - In a large pot, combine vegetable or chicken broth and water. Bring to a simmer over medium heat.
3. **Add Vegetables:**
    - Add thinly sliced red bell pepper and shredded cabbage or coleslaw mix to the simmering broth. Cook for about 3-5 minutes until vegetables are tender-crisp.
4. **Cook the Noodles:**
    - Cook the ramen noodles according to package instructions. Drain and rinse under cold water to stop cooking. Divide noodles among serving bowls.
5. **Assemble the Ramen Bowls:**
    - Ladle the hot broth and vegetables over the noodles in each bowl.
6. **Add Peanut Sauce:**
    - Stir the prepared spicy peanut sauce into the broth, ensuring it's well combined. Taste and adjust seasoning with salt and pepper if needed.
7. **Garnish and Serve:**
    - Garnish each bowl with sliced scallions (green onions), crushed peanuts, and a lime wedge for squeezing over the ramen.

8. **Serve Immediately:**
    - Serve hot and enjoy your Spicy Peanut Ramen!

This recipe serves 4. Adjust quantities based on your preference and enjoy the creamy, spicy, and nutty flavors of this delicious Spicy Peanut Ramen!

Vegetable Tofu Ramen

Ingredients:

- 4 packs of fresh ramen noodles (or dried, follow package instructions)
- 6 cups vegetable broth
- 2 cups water
- 1 block firm tofu, cut into cubes
- 2 tablespoons soy sauce (or tamari for gluten-free)
- 1 tablespoon miso paste
- 1 tablespoon sesame oil
- 1 tablespoon grated ginger
- 2 cloves garlic, minced
- 1 tablespoon vegetable oil
- 1 cup sliced shiitake mushrooms
- 1 cup thinly sliced carrots
- 1 cup sliced bell peppers (red, yellow, or green)
- 2 cups baby spinach or chopped kale
- Salt and pepper to taste
- Thinly sliced green onions (for garnish)
- Sesame seeds (for garnish, optional)
- Nori (seaweed sheets), cut into strips (optional)
- Soft-boiled eggs (optional, for topping)

Instructions:

1. **Prepare the Tofu:**
   - Heat vegetable oil in a large skillet or frying pan over medium-high heat. Add tofu cubes and cook until golden brown on all sides. Remove from heat and set aside.
2. **Make the Broth:**
   - In a large pot, combine vegetable broth and water. Bring to a simmer over medium heat.
3. **Add Flavorings:**
   - Stir in soy sauce, miso paste, sesame oil, grated ginger, and minced garlic. Simmer for about 5 minutes to allow flavors to meld. Taste and adjust seasoning with salt and pepper if needed.
4. **Cook the Vegetables:**
   - Add sliced shiitake mushrooms, thinly sliced carrots, and sliced bell peppers to the simmering broth. Cook for about 3-5 minutes until vegetables are tender-crisp.
5. **Cook the Noodles:**
   - Cook the ramen noodles according to package instructions. Drain and rinse under cold water to stop cooking. Divide noodles among serving bowls.
6. **Assemble the Ramen Bowls:**
   - Ladle the hot broth and vegetables over the noodles in each bowl.

7. **Add Tofu and Greens:**
   - Add cooked tofu cubes and baby spinach or chopped kale to each bowl of ramen.
8. **Garnish and Serve:**
   - Garnish with thinly sliced green onions, sesame seeds (if using), nori strips (if using), and soft-boiled eggs (if using) if desired.
9. **Serve Immediately:**
   - Serve hot and enjoy your comforting Vegetable Tofu Ramen!

This recipe serves 4. Adjust quantities based on your preference and enjoy the wholesome and nourishing flavors of this Vegetable Tofu Ramen!

Scallion Beef Ramen

Ingredients:

- 4 packs of fresh ramen noodles (or dried, follow package instructions)
- 6 cups beef broth
- 2 cups water
- 1 lb beef sirloin or flank steak, thinly sliced
- 1 cup chopped scallions (green onions), divided (white and green parts separated)
- 2 tablespoons soy sauce
- 1 tablespoon oyster sauce
- 1 tablespoon sesame oil
- 1 tablespoon rice vinegar
- 2 cloves garlic, minced
- 1 tablespoon grated ginger
- 1 tablespoon vegetable oil
- Salt and pepper to taste
- Soft-boiled eggs (optional, for topping)
- Nori (seaweed sheets), cut into strips (optional, for garnish)
- Red chili flakes or chili oil (optional, for heat)

Instructions:

1. **Marinate the Beef:**
    - In a bowl, combine soy sauce, oyster sauce, sesame oil, rice vinegar, minced garlic, grated ginger, and the white parts of chopped scallions. Add the thinly sliced beef and toss to coat. Marinate for at least 15-20 minutes.
2. **Cook the Beef:**
    - Heat vegetable oil in a large skillet or wok over medium-high heat. Add the marinated beef (reserving the marinade) and stir-fry for 2-3 minutes until beef is browned and cooked through. Remove beef from the skillet and set aside.
3. **Make the Broth:**
    - In the same skillet or wok, pour in beef broth and water. Bring to a simmer over medium heat.
4. **Add Flavorings:**
    - Stir in the reserved marinade and simmer for about 5 minutes to infuse the flavors into the broth. Taste and adjust seasoning with salt and pepper if needed.
5. **Cook the Noodles:**
    - Cook the ramen noodles according to package instructions. Drain and rinse under cold water to stop cooking. Divide noodles among serving bowls.
6. **Assemble the Ramen Bowls:**
    - Ladle the hot broth over the noodles in each bowl.
7. **Add Beef and Scallions:**
    - Top each bowl with the cooked beef slices and the remaining chopped scallions (green parts).

8. **Garnish and Serve:**
    - Garnish with soft-boiled eggs (if using), nori strips (if using), and red chili flakes or chili oil (if using) for added heat.
9. **Serve Immediately:**
    - Serve hot and enjoy your flavorful Scallion Beef Ramen!

This recipe serves 4. Adjust quantities based on your preference and enjoy the delicious combination of beef, scallions, and savory broth in this Scallion Beef Ramen!

Sichuan Dan Dan Noodles

Ingredients:

For the Sauce:

- 2 tablespoons sesame paste (or tahini)
- 2 tablespoons soy sauce
- 1 tablespoon rice vinegar
- 1 tablespoon chili oil (adjust to taste)
- 1 teaspoon Sichuan peppercorn powder (adjust to taste)
- 1 teaspoon sugar
- 2 cloves garlic, minced
- 1 tablespoon grated ginger
- 1/4 cup chicken or vegetable broth

For the Noodles:

- 4 packs of fresh Chinese egg noodles (or use ramen noodles)
- 1/2 lb ground pork (optional, for meat version)
- 2 tablespoons vegetable oil
- 2 tablespoons soy sauce
- 2 tablespoons Shaoxing wine (or dry sherry)
- 2 cups baby spinach or Chinese greens, blanched (optional, for serving)
- Thinly sliced green onions (for garnish)
- Chopped roasted peanuts (for garnish)
- Fresh cilantro leaves (for garnish, optional)

Instructions:

1. **Prepare the Sauce:**
    - In a bowl, whisk together sesame paste (or tahini), soy sauce, rice vinegar, chili oil, Sichuan peppercorn powder, sugar, minced garlic, grated ginger, and chicken or vegetable broth. Adjust chili oil and Sichuan peppercorn powder to your desired level of spiciness and numbness.
2. **Cook the Noodles:**
    - Cook the noodles according to package instructions. Drain and set aside.
3. **Cook the Ground Pork (optional):**
    - Heat vegetable oil in a large skillet or wok over medium-high heat. Add ground pork and cook until browned and cooked through. Drain excess fat if needed.
4. **Combine Noodles and Sauce:**
    - In a large mixing bowl, toss cooked noodles with the prepared sauce until well coated. Add cooked ground pork (if using) and toss again.
5. **Serve:**

- Divide the noodles among serving bowls. Top with blanched baby spinach or Chinese greens (if using), thinly sliced green onions, chopped roasted peanuts, and fresh cilantro leaves (if using).
6. **Enjoy:**
    - Serve immediately and enjoy the bold and spicy flavors of Sichuan Dan Dan Noodles!

This recipe serves 4. Adjust quantities based on your preference and enjoy this authentic and flavorful Sichuan dish right at home!

Char Siu Ramen

Ingredients:

For the Char Siu (Marinated Pork):

- 1 lb pork belly or pork shoulder, thinly sliced
- 3 tablespoons soy sauce
- 2 tablespoons hoisin sauce
- 2 tablespoons honey or brown sugar
- 1 tablespoon Chinese rice wine (Shaoxing wine) or dry sherry
- 1 tablespoon sesame oil
- 1 tablespoon grated ginger
- 2 cloves garlic, minced
- 1 teaspoon five-spice powder
- Salt and pepper to taste

For the Ramen:

- 4 packs of fresh ramen noodles (or dried, follow package instructions)
- 6 cups chicken or pork broth
- 2 cups water
- 2 tablespoons soy sauce (or to taste)
- 1 tablespoon mirin (Japanese sweet rice wine)
- 1 tablespoon sesame oil
- 1 tablespoon miso paste (optional, for added depth of flavor)
- 1 tablespoon grated ginger
- 2 cloves garlic, minced
- Salt and pepper to taste
- Thinly sliced green onions (for garnish)
- Soft-boiled eggs (optional, for topping)
- Nori (seaweed sheets), cut into strips (optional, for garnish)
- Red chili flakes or chili oil (optional, for heat)

Instructions:

Prepare the Char Siu (Marinated Pork):

1. In a bowl, combine soy sauce, hoisin sauce, honey or brown sugar, Chinese rice wine (or dry sherry), sesame oil, grated ginger, minced garlic, five-spice powder, salt, and pepper. Mix well.
2. Place the thinly sliced pork into a large resealable plastic bag or shallow dish. Pour the marinade over the pork, ensuring it's evenly coated. Marinate in the refrigerator for at least 2 hours, or ideally overnight.
3. Preheat the oven to 375°F (190°C). Line a baking sheet with aluminum foil and place a wire rack on top. Arrange the marinated pork slices on the rack.

4. Bake for 20-25 minutes, turning halfway through, or until the pork is cooked through and caramelized on the edges. Remove from the oven and let it rest for a few minutes before slicing thinly.

Make the Ramen:

1. In a large pot, combine chicken or pork broth and water. Bring to a simmer over medium heat.
2. Stir in soy sauce, mirin, sesame oil, miso paste (if using), grated ginger, minced garlic, salt, and pepper. Simmer for about 5-10 minutes to allow the flavors to meld. Taste and adjust seasoning if needed.
3. Cook the ramen noodles according to package instructions. Drain and rinse under cold water to stop cooking. Divide noodles among serving bowls.
4. Ladle the hot broth over the noodles in each bowl.
5. Arrange slices of char siu pork on top of each bowl of ramen.
6. Garnish with thinly sliced green onions, soft-boiled eggs (if using), nori strips (if using), and red chili flakes or chili oil (if using) for added heat.
7. Serve immediately and enjoy your homemade Char Siu Ramen!

This recipe serves 4. Adjust quantities based on your preference and enjoy the delicious combination of tender char siu pork and savory ramen noodles in a flavorful broth!

Chicken and Mushroom Ramen

Ingredients:

- 4 packs of fresh ramen noodles (or dried, follow package instructions)
- 6 cups chicken broth
- 2 cups water
- 2 boneless, skinless chicken breasts, thinly sliced
- 2 cups sliced mushrooms (shiitake, cremini, or your choice)
- 1 cup sliced bamboo shoots (optional)
- 2 tablespoons soy sauce (or tamari for gluten-free)
- 1 tablespoon sesame oil
- 1 tablespoon grated ginger
- 2 cloves garlic, minced
- 1 tablespoon miso paste (optional, for added depth of flavor)
- Salt and pepper to taste
- Thinly sliced green onions (for garnish)
- Soft-boiled eggs (optional, for topping)
- Nori (seaweed sheets), cut into strips (optional, for garnish)
- Red chili flakes or chili oil (optional, for heat)

Instructions:

1. **Cook the Chicken:**
   - In a large pot, bring chicken broth and water to a boil. Add thinly sliced chicken breasts and cook for about 5-7 minutes, or until chicken is cooked through. Remove chicken from the pot and set aside.
2. **Prepare the Broth:**
   - In the same pot with the chicken broth, add sliced mushrooms, bamboo shoots (if using), soy sauce, sesame oil, grated ginger, minced garlic, and miso paste (if using). Bring to a simmer over medium heat.
3. **Cook the Noodles:**
   - Cook the ramen noodles according to package instructions. Drain and rinse under cold water to stop cooking. Divide noodles among serving bowls.
4. **Assemble the Ramen Bowls:**
   - Ladle the hot broth with mushrooms and bamboo shoots over the noodles in each bowl.
5. **Add Chicken and Garnish:**
   - Top each bowl with the thinly sliced cooked chicken.
6. **Garnish and Serve:**
   - Garnish with thinly sliced green onions, soft-boiled eggs (if using), nori strips (if using), and red chili flakes or chili oil (if using) for added heat.
7. **Serve Immediately:**
   - Serve hot and enjoy your comforting Chicken and Mushroom Ramen!

This recipe serves 4. Adjust quantities based on your preference and enjoy the delicious combination of chicken, mushrooms, and savory broth in this Chicken and Mushroom Ramen!

Braised Chicken Ramen

Ingredients:

For Braised Chicken:

- 4 bone-in, skin-on chicken thighs
- Salt and pepper to taste
- 1 tablespoon vegetable oil
- 1 onion, chopped
- 2 carrots, chopped
- 2 celery stalks, chopped
- 4 cloves garlic, minced
- 1 tablespoon tomato paste
- 1 tablespoon soy sauce
- 1 tablespoon Worcestershire sauce
- 4 cups chicken broth
- 2 cups water
- 1 bay leaf
- 1 teaspoon dried thyme
- 1 teaspoon dried rosemary
- 1 teaspoon paprika
- Fresh parsley, chopped (for garnish)

For Ramen:

- 4 packs of fresh ramen noodles (or dried, follow package instructions)
- 6 cups chicken broth (additional, for ramen base)
- 2 cups water (additional, for ramen base)
- 1 tablespoon soy sauce
- 1 tablespoon sesame oil
- 1 tablespoon miso paste (optional, for added depth of flavor)
- 1 tablespoon grated ginger
- Salt and pepper to taste
- Thinly sliced green onions (for garnish)
- Soft-boiled eggs (optional, for topping)
- Nori (seaweed sheets), cut into strips (optional, for garnish)
- Red chili flakes or chili oil (optional, for heat)

Instructions:

Prepare Braised Chicken:

1. Season chicken thighs with salt and pepper.

2. Heat vegetable oil in a large Dutch oven or heavy-bottomed pot over medium-high heat. Add chicken thighs, skin side down, and cook until golden brown, about 5-6 minutes per side. Remove chicken from the pot and set aside.
3. In the same pot, add chopped onion, carrots, and celery. Cook until vegetables are softened, about 5 minutes.
4. Add minced garlic, tomato paste, soy sauce, and Worcestershire sauce. Cook for another 1-2 minutes, stirring frequently.
5. Return chicken thighs to the pot. Pour in chicken broth and water. Add bay leaf, dried thyme, dried rosemary, and paprika. Bring to a simmer.
6. Cover and cook over low heat for 30-40 minutes, or until chicken is cooked through and tender. Remove chicken thighs from the pot and set aside to cool slightly. Once cooled, shred the chicken meat and discard the bones and skin.
7. Strain the braising liquid through a fine mesh sieve, discarding the solids. Return the strained liquid (broth) to the pot and keep warm over low heat.

Prepare Ramen:

1. In a separate large pot, combine chicken broth and water. Bring to a simmer over medium heat.
2. Stir in soy sauce, sesame oil, miso paste (if using), grated ginger, salt, and pepper. Simmer for about 5 minutes to allow flavors to meld. Taste and adjust seasoning if needed.
3. Cook the ramen noodles according to package instructions. Drain and rinse under cold water to stop cooking. Divide noodles among serving bowls.
4. Ladle the hot broth over the noodles in each bowl.
5. Add shredded braised chicken meat to each bowl of ramen.
6. Garnish with thinly sliced green onions, soft-boiled eggs (if using), nori strips (if using), and red chili flakes or chili oil (if using) for added heat.
7. Sprinkle with chopped fresh parsley for garnish.
8. Serve immediately and enjoy your comforting Braised Chicken Ramen!

This recipe serves 4. Adjust quantities based on your preference and enjoy the rich and comforting flavors of Braised Chicken Ramen!

Spicy Garlic Ramen

Ingredients:

- 4 packs of fresh ramen noodles (or dried, follow package instructions)
- 6 cups chicken or vegetable broth
- 2 cups water
- 4 cloves garlic, minced
- 1 tablespoon grated ginger
- 2 tablespoons soy sauce (or tamari for gluten-free)
- 1 tablespoon sesame oil
- 1 tablespoon chili garlic sauce (adjust to taste)
- 1 tablespoon sriracha sauce (adjust to taste)
- 1 tablespoon rice vinegar
- 1 tablespoon brown sugar
- Salt and pepper to taste
- Thinly sliced green onions (for garnish)
- Soft-boiled eggs (optional, for topping)
- Nori (seaweed sheets), cut into strips (optional, for garnish)
- Red chili flakes or chili oil (optional, for extra heat)

Instructions:

1. **Prepare the Broth:**
   - In a large pot, combine chicken or vegetable broth and water. Bring to a simmer over medium heat.
2. **Add Flavorings:**
   - Stir in minced garlic, grated ginger, soy sauce, sesame oil, chili garlic sauce, sriracha sauce, rice vinegar, and brown sugar. Simmer for about 5-10 minutes to allow the flavors to meld. Taste and adjust seasoning with salt and pepper if needed.
3. **Cook the Noodles:**
   - Cook the ramen noodles according to package instructions. Drain and rinse under cold water to stop cooking. Divide noodles among serving bowls.
4. **Assemble the Ramen Bowls:**
   - Ladle the hot spicy garlic broth over the noodles in each bowl.
5. **Garnish and Serve:**
   - Garnish each bowl with thinly sliced green onions, soft-boiled eggs (if using), nori strips (if using), and red chili flakes or chili oil (if using) for extra heat.
6. **Serve Immediately:**
   - Serve hot and enjoy your Spicy Garlic Ramen!

This recipe serves 4. Adjust quantities based on your preference and enjoy the bold and spicy flavors of Spicy Garlic Ramen!

Spicy Sesame Ramen

Ingredients:

- 4 packs of fresh ramen noodles (or dried, follow package instructions)
- 6 cups chicken or vegetable broth
- 2 cups water
- 3 tablespoons sesame paste (tahini)
- 2 tablespoons soy sauce (or tamari for gluten-free)
- 1 tablespoon sesame oil
- 1 tablespoon chili garlic sauce (adjust to taste)
- 1 tablespoon rice vinegar
- 1 tablespoon brown sugar
- 2 cloves garlic, minced
- 1 tablespoon grated ginger
- Salt and pepper to taste
- Thinly sliced green onions (for garnish)
- Soft-boiled eggs (optional, for topping)
- Nori (seaweed sheets), cut into strips (optional, for garnish)
- Red chili flakes or chili oil (optional, for extra heat)

Instructions:

1. **Prepare the Broth:**
   - In a large pot, combine chicken or vegetable broth and water. Bring to a simmer over medium heat.
2. **Make the Sesame Sauce:**
   - In a small bowl, whisk together sesame paste (tahini), soy sauce, sesame oil, chili garlic sauce, rice vinegar, brown sugar, minced garlic, and grated ginger until smooth.
3. **Add Flavorings:**
   - Stir the sesame sauce mixture into the simmering broth. Simmer for about 5-10 minutes to allow the flavors to meld. Taste and adjust seasoning with salt and pepper if needed.
4. **Cook the Noodles:**
   - Cook the ramen noodles according to package instructions. Drain and rinse under cold water to stop cooking. Divide noodles among serving bowls.
5. **Assemble the Ramen Bowls:**
   - Ladle the hot spicy sesame broth over the noodles in each bowl.
6. **Garnish and Serve:**
   - Garnish each bowl with thinly sliced green onions, soft-boiled eggs (if using), nori strips (if using), and red chili flakes or chili oil (if using) for extra heat.
7. **Serve Immediately:**
   - Serve hot and enjoy your Spicy Sesame Ramen!

This recipe serves 4. Adjust quantities based on your preference and enjoy the nutty, spicy flavors of Spicy Sesame Ramen!

Pork Rib Ramen

Ingredients:

For the Pork Ribs:

- 2 lbs pork ribs (baby back or spare ribs)
- Salt and pepper to taste
- 1 tablespoon vegetable oil

For the Ramen Broth:

- 6 cups chicken or pork broth
- 2 cups water
- 2 tablespoons soy sauce (or tamari for gluten-free)
- 1 tablespoon sake (Japanese rice wine) or dry sherry
- 1 tablespoon mirin (Japanese sweet rice wine)
- 2 cloves garlic, minced
- 1 tablespoon grated ginger
- 2 green onions, chopped
- 1 tablespoon miso paste (optional, for added depth of flavor)
- Salt and pepper to taste

For Serving:

- 4 packs of fresh ramen noodles (or dried, follow package instructions)
- Thinly sliced green onions (for garnish)
- Soft-boiled eggs (optional, for topping)
- Nori (seaweed sheets), cut into strips (optional, for garnish)
- Red chili flakes or chili oil (optional, for heat)

Instructions:

Prepare the Pork Ribs:

1. Season the pork ribs generously with salt and pepper.
2. Heat vegetable oil in a large pot or Dutch oven over medium-high heat. Add the pork ribs and sear until browned on all sides, about 5-7 minutes. Remove ribs from the pot and set aside.

Make the Ramen Broth:

1. In the same pot, add chicken or pork broth, water, soy sauce, sake (or dry sherry), mirin, minced garlic, grated ginger, and chopped green onions. Stir to combine.
2. If using miso paste, dissolve it in a small amount of the broth before adding it to the pot for better incorporation.

3. Return the seared pork ribs to the pot. Bring the broth to a boil, then reduce heat to low. Cover and simmer for 1.5 to 2 hours, or until the pork ribs are tender and falling off the bone.
4. Remove the pork ribs from the broth and set aside. Strain the broth through a fine mesh sieve, discarding any solids. Skim off excess fat from the broth if desired.

Prepare the Noodles and Assemble:

1. Cook the ramen noodles according to package instructions. Drain and rinse under cold water to stop cooking. Divide noodles among serving bowls.
2. Ladle the hot broth over the noodles in each bowl.
3. Add one or two pork ribs to each bowl of ramen.
4. Garnish with thinly sliced green onions, soft-boiled eggs (if using), nori strips (if using), and red chili flakes or chili oil (if using) for extra heat.
5. Serve immediately and enjoy your Pork Rib Ramen!

This recipe serves 4. Adjust quantities based on your preference and enjoy the hearty and flavorful Pork Rib Ramen!

Spinach and Egg Ramen

Ingredients:

- 4 packs of fresh ramen noodles (or dried, follow package instructions)
- 6 cups chicken or vegetable broth
- 2 cups water
- 4 eggs
- 4 cups fresh spinach leaves, washed and trimmed
- 2 tablespoons soy sauce (or tamari for gluten-free)
- 1 tablespoon sesame oil
- 1 tablespoon rice vinegar
- 2 cloves garlic, minced
- 1 tablespoon grated ginger
- Salt and pepper to taste
- Thinly sliced green onions (for garnish)
- Nori (seaweed sheets), cut into strips (optional, for garnish)
- Red chili flakes or chili oil (optional, for heat)

Instructions:

1. **Prepare Soft-Boiled Eggs:**
   - Bring a pot of water to a boil. Carefully add eggs using a slotted spoon. Reduce heat to a gentle simmer and cook eggs for 7 minutes. Remove eggs and place them in a bowl of ice water to cool. Once cool, peel and set aside.
2. **Prepare the Broth:**
   - In a large pot, combine chicken or vegetable broth and water. Bring to a simmer over medium heat.
3. **Add Flavorings:**
   - Stir in soy sauce, sesame oil, rice vinegar, minced garlic, grated ginger, salt, and pepper. Simmer for about 5 minutes to allow flavors to meld. Taste and adjust seasoning if needed.
4. **Cook the Noodles:**
   - Cook the ramen noodles according to package instructions. Drain and rinse under cold water to stop cooking. Divide noodles among serving bowls.
5. **Blanch Spinach:**
   - In the same pot of boiling water used for eggs (or a separate pot), blanch spinach for 1-2 minutes until wilted. Remove spinach with a slotted spoon and rinse under cold water. Squeeze out excess water and divide spinach among serving bowls.
6. **Assemble the Ramen Bowls:**
   - Ladle the hot broth over the noodles and spinach in each bowl.
7. **Slice and Garnish Eggs:**
   - Slice the soft-boiled eggs in half and place one half in each bowl of ramen.
8. **Garnish and Serve:**

- Garnish each bowl with thinly sliced green onions, nori strips (if using), and red chili flakes or chili oil (if using) for added flavor and heat.
9. **Serve Immediately:**
    - Serve hot and enjoy your nutritious and comforting Spinach and Egg Ramen!

This recipe serves 4. Adjust quantities based on your preference and enjoy the wholesome combination of spinach, eggs, and savory broth in this Spinach and Egg Ramen!

Beef Shank Ramen

Ingredients:

For the Beef Shank:

- 2 lbs beef shank, preferably bone-in
- Salt and pepper to taste
- 2 tablespoons vegetable oil

For the Ramen Broth:

- 6 cups beef broth
- 2 cups water
- 1 onion, chopped
- 2 carrots, chopped
- 2 celery stalks, chopped
- 4 cloves garlic, minced
- 1 tablespoon grated ginger
- 2 tablespoons soy sauce (or tamari for gluten-free)
- 1 tablespoon mirin (Japanese sweet rice wine)
- 1 tablespoon sesame oil
- Salt and pepper to taste

For Serving:

- 4 packs of fresh ramen noodles (or dried, follow package instructions)
- Thinly sliced green onions (for garnish)
- Soft-boiled eggs (optional, for topping)
- Nori (seaweed sheets), cut into strips (optional, for garnish)
- Red chili flakes or chili oil (optional, for heat)

Instructions:

Prepare the Beef Shank:

1. Season the beef shank with salt and pepper.
2. Heat vegetable oil in a large pot or Dutch oven over medium-high heat. Add the beef shank and sear until browned on all sides, about 5-7 minutes. Remove beef shank from the pot and set aside.

Make the Ramen Broth:

1. In the same pot, add chopped onion, carrots, and celery. Cook until vegetables are softened, about 5 minutes.

2. Add minced garlic, grated ginger, soy sauce, mirin, sesame oil, beef broth, and water. Stir to combine.
3. Return the seared beef shank to the pot. Bring the broth to a boil, then reduce heat to low. Cover and simmer for 2.5 to 3 hours, or until the beef shank is tender and falling off the bone.
4. Remove the beef shank from the broth and set aside. Strain the broth through a fine mesh sieve, discarding any solids. Skim off excess fat from the broth if desired.

Prepare the Noodles and Assemble:

1. Cook the ramen noodles according to package instructions. Drain and rinse under cold water to stop cooking. Divide noodles among serving bowls.
2. Ladle the hot broth over the noodles in each bowl.
3. Slice the beef shank into thin slices and place on top of each bowl of ramen.
4. Garnish with thinly sliced green onions, soft-boiled eggs (if using), nori strips (if using), and red chili flakes or chili oil (if using) for added heat.
5. Serve immediately and enjoy your Beef Shank Ramen!

This recipe serves 4. Adjust quantities based on your preference and enjoy the rich and satisfying flavors of Beef Shank Ramen!

XO Sauce Seafood Ramen

Ingredients:

For the XO Sauce:

- 1/2 cup dried shrimp, soaked in hot water for 15 minutes and drained
- 1/2 cup dried scallops, soaked in hot water for 15 minutes and drained
- 1/2 cup dried Chinese ham or bacon, finely chopped
- 1/2 cup shallots, finely chopped
- 1/4 cup garlic, finely chopped
- 1/4 cup vegetable oil
- 2 tablespoons chili garlic sauce or chopped dried chili peppers (adjust to taste)
- 2 tablespoons soy sauce
- 1 tablespoon oyster sauce
- 1 tablespoon Shaoxing wine or dry sherry
- 1 tablespoon sugar
- Salt to taste

For the Ramen:

- 4 packs of fresh ramen noodles (or dried, follow package instructions)
- 6 cups seafood or chicken broth
- 2 cups water
- 1 lb mixed seafood (such as shrimp, squid, and scallops), cleaned and cut into bite-sized pieces
- 2 cups baby spinach or Chinese greens, washed and trimmed
- 2 tablespoons soy sauce (or tamari for gluten-free)
- 1 tablespoon sesame oil
- 1 tablespoon rice vinegar
- 2 cloves garlic, minced
- 1 tablespoon grated ginger
- Salt and pepper to taste
- Thinly sliced green onions (for garnish)
- Nori (seaweed sheets), cut into strips (optional, for garnish)
- Red chili flakes or chili oil (optional, for heat)

Instructions:

Prepare the XO Sauce:

1. In a food processor, pulse the soaked dried shrimp and scallops until finely chopped.
2. Heat vegetable oil in a large skillet or wok over medium heat. Add Chinese ham or bacon and cook until lightly browned and crispy.
3. Add shallots and garlic to the skillet. Cook until softened and aromatic, about 2-3 minutes.

4. Stir in the chopped dried shrimp and scallops, chili garlic sauce (or chopped dried chili peppers), soy sauce, oyster sauce, Shaoxing wine (or dry sherry), and sugar. Cook, stirring frequently, until the mixture is well combined and fragrant, about 5-7 minutes. Season with salt to taste. Remove from heat and set aside.

Make the Ramen:

1. In a large pot, combine seafood or chicken broth and water. Bring to a simmer over medium heat.
2. Stir in soy sauce, sesame oil, rice vinegar, minced garlic, grated ginger, salt, and pepper. Simmer for about 5 minutes to allow flavors to meld. Taste and adjust seasoning if needed.
3. Add mixed seafood to the broth and simmer until cooked through, about 2-3 minutes. Add baby spinach or Chinese greens and cook for another minute until wilted.
4. Cook the ramen noodles according to package instructions. Drain and rinse under cold water to stop cooking. Divide noodles among serving bowls.
5. Ladle the hot seafood broth over the noodles in each bowl.
6. Spoon XO sauce over the seafood and broth in each bowl.
7. Garnish with thinly sliced green onions, nori strips (if using), and red chili flakes or chili oil (if using) for added heat.
8. Serve immediately and enjoy your XO Sauce Seafood Ramen!

This recipe serves 4. Adjust quantities based on your preference and enjoy the bold flavors of XO Sauce Seafood Ramen!

Cumin Lamb Ramen

Ingredients:

For the Cumin Lamb:

- 1 lb lamb leg or shoulder, thinly sliced
- 2 tablespoons soy sauce
- 1 tablespoon Shaoxing wine or dry sherry
- 1 tablespoon cornstarch
- 1 tablespoon vegetable oil
- 2 tablespoons cumin seeds
- 1 teaspoon Sichuan peppercorns (optional, for a numbing sensation)
- 4 cloves garlic, minced
- 1 tablespoon grated ginger
- 2 green onions, sliced
- Salt and pepper to taste

For the Ramen:

- 4 packs of fresh ramen noodles (or dried, follow package instructions)
- 6 cups beef or chicken broth
- 2 cups water
- 1 tablespoon soy sauce (or tamari for gluten-free)
- 1 tablespoon sesame oil
- 1 tablespoon rice vinegar
- 1 tablespoon miso paste (optional, for added depth of flavor)
- Thinly sliced green onions (for garnish)
- Soft-boiled eggs (optional, for topping)
- Nori (seaweed sheets), cut into strips (optional, for garnish)
- Red chili flakes or chili oil (optional, for heat)

Instructions:

Prepare the Cumin Lamb:

1. In a bowl, combine soy sauce, Shaoxing wine (or dry sherry), and cornstarch. Add sliced lamb and marinate for 15-20 minutes.
2. Heat vegetable oil in a large skillet or wok over medium-high heat. Add cumin seeds and Sichuan peppercorns (if using). Toast for 1-2 minutes until fragrant.
3. Add minced garlic, grated ginger, and sliced green onions to the skillet. Stir-fry for about 1 minute until aromatic.
4. Add marinated lamb slices to the skillet. Stir-fry for 3-4 minutes until lamb is browned and cooked through. Season with salt and pepper to taste. Remove from heat and set aside.

Make the Ramen:

1. In a large pot, combine beef or chicken broth and water. Bring to a simmer over medium heat.
2. Stir in soy sauce, sesame oil, rice vinegar, and miso paste (if using). Simmer for about 5 minutes to allow flavors to meld. Taste and adjust seasoning if needed.
3. Cook the ramen noodles according to package instructions. Drain and rinse under cold water to stop cooking. Divide noodles among serving bowls.
4. Ladle the hot broth over the noodles in each bowl.
5. Top each bowl with the cumin-spiced lamb slices.
6. Garnish with thinly sliced green onions, soft-boiled eggs (if using), nori strips (if using), and red chili flakes or chili oil (if using) for added heat.
7. Serve immediately and enjoy your Cumin Lamb Ramen!

This recipe serves 4. Adjust quantities based on your preference and enjoy the aromatic and flavorful Cumin Lamb Ramen!

Pickled Vegetables Ramen

Ingredients:

For the Pickled Vegetables:

- 2 cups thinly sliced vegetables (such as carrots, daikon radish, cucumber, or cabbage)
- 1 cup rice vinegar
- 1/2 cup water
- 1/4 cup sugar
- 1 teaspoon salt

For the Ramen:

- 4 packs of fresh ramen noodles (or dried, follow package instructions)
- 6 cups vegetable or mushroom broth (for vegetarian version) or chicken broth
- 2 cups water
- 2 tablespoons soy sauce (or tamari for gluten-free)
- 1 tablespoon sesame oil
- 1 tablespoon rice vinegar
- 2 cloves garlic, minced
- 1 tablespoon grated ginger
- Salt and pepper to taste
- Thinly sliced green onions (for garnish)
- Soft-boiled eggs (optional, for topping)
- Nori (seaweed sheets), cut into strips (optional, for garnish)
- Red chili flakes or chili oil (optional, for heat)

Instructions:

Prepare the Pickled Vegetables:

1. In a small saucepan, combine rice vinegar, water, sugar, and salt. Bring to a simmer over medium heat, stirring until sugar and salt dissolve.
2. Remove from heat and let the pickling liquid cool slightly.
3. Place thinly sliced vegetables in a glass or ceramic bowl. Pour the warm pickling liquid over the vegetables, ensuring they are completely submerged.
4. Cover and refrigerate for at least 1 hour, or preferably overnight, to allow the flavors to develop.

Make the Ramen:

1. In a large pot, combine vegetable or mushroom broth and water. Bring to a simmer over medium heat.

2. Stir in soy sauce, sesame oil, rice vinegar, minced garlic, grated ginger, salt, and pepper. Simmer for about 5 minutes to allow flavors to meld. Taste and adjust seasoning if needed.
3. Cook the ramen noodles according to package instructions. Drain and rinse under cold water to stop cooking. Divide noodles among serving bowls.
4. Ladle the hot broth over the noodles in each bowl.
5. Top each bowl with a generous serving of pickled vegetables.
6. Garnish with thinly sliced green onions, soft-boiled eggs (if using), nori strips (if using), and red chili flakes or chili oil (if using) for added heat.
7. Serve immediately and enjoy your Pickled Vegetables Ramen!

This recipe serves 4. Adjust quantities based on your preference and enjoy the tangy crunch of Pickled Vegetables Ramen!

Pork and Cabbage Ramen

Ingredients:

For the Pork:

- 1 lb pork shoulder or pork belly, thinly sliced
- 2 tablespoons soy sauce
- 1 tablespoon mirin (Japanese sweet rice wine) or dry sherry
- 1 tablespoon vegetable oil

For the Ramen Broth:

- 6 cups pork or chicken broth
- 2 cups water
- 2 tablespoons soy sauce (or tamari for gluten-free)
- 1 tablespoon sesame oil
- 2 cloves garlic, minced
- 1 tablespoon grated ginger
- Salt and pepper to taste

Additional Ingredients:

- 4 packs of fresh ramen noodles (or dried, follow package instructions)
- 4 cups shredded cabbage
- Thinly sliced green onions (for garnish)
- Soft-boiled eggs (optional, for topping)
- Nori (seaweed sheets), cut into strips (optional, for garnish)
- Red chili flakes or chili oil (optional, for heat)

Instructions:

Prepare the Pork:

1. In a bowl, combine thinly sliced pork with soy sauce and mirin (or dry sherry). Marinate for 15-20 minutes.
2. Heat vegetable oil in a large skillet or wok over medium-high heat. Add marinated pork slices and cook until browned and cooked through, about 3-4 minutes. Remove pork from skillet and set aside.

Make the Ramen Broth:

1. In a large pot, combine pork or chicken broth and water. Bring to a simmer over medium heat.
2. Stir in soy sauce, sesame oil, minced garlic, grated ginger, salt, and pepper. Simmer for about 5 minutes to allow flavors to meld. Taste and adjust seasoning if needed.

Prepare the Ramen Noodles and Cabbage:

1. Cook the ramen noodles according to package instructions. Drain and rinse under cold water to stop cooking. Divide noodles among serving bowls.
2. In the same pot of boiling water used for noodles, blanch shredded cabbage for 1-2 minutes until slightly tender. Drain and divide among serving bowls.

Assemble the Ramen Bowls:

1. Ladle the hot broth over the noodles and cabbage in each bowl.
2. Top each bowl with cooked pork slices.
3. Garnish with thinly sliced green onions, soft-boiled eggs (if using), nori strips (if using), and red chili flakes or chili oil (if using) for added heat.
4. Serve immediately and enjoy your Pork and Cabbage Ramen!

This recipe serves 4. Adjust quantities based on your preference and enjoy the comforting flavors of Pork and Cabbage Ramen!

Soy Sauce Chicken Ramen

Ingredients:

For the Soy Sauce Chicken:

- 4 boneless, skinless chicken thighs
- 1/2 cup soy sauce
- 1/4 cup mirin (Japanese sweet rice wine) or dry sherry
- 2 tablespoons brown sugar
- 2 cloves garlic, minced
- 1 tablespoon grated ginger
- 1 tablespoon vegetable oil

For the Ramen Broth:

- 6 cups chicken broth
- 2 cups water
- 2 tablespoons soy sauce (or tamari for gluten-free)
- 1 tablespoon sesame oil
- 2 cloves garlic, minced
- 1 tablespoon grated ginger
- Salt and pepper to taste

Additional Ingredients:

- 4 packs of fresh ramen noodles (or dried, follow package instructions)
- Baby spinach or Chinese greens, washed and trimmed
- Thinly sliced green onions (for garnish)
- Soft-boiled eggs (optional, for topping)
- Nori (seaweed sheets), cut into strips (optional, for garnish)
- Red chili flakes or chili oil (optional, for heat)

Instructions:

Prepare the Soy Sauce Chicken:

1. In a bowl, combine soy sauce, mirin (or dry sherry), brown sugar, minced garlic, and grated ginger. Stir until sugar is dissolved.
2. Add chicken thighs to the marinade, ensuring they are well coated. Marinate for at least 30 minutes, or preferably up to 2 hours in the refrigerator.
3. Heat vegetable oil in a large skillet or frying pan over medium-high heat. Remove chicken from marinade (reserve marinade) and cook until browned on both sides and cooked through, about 6-8 minutes per side. Remove chicken from skillet and let it rest for a few minutes before slicing thinly.

Make the Ramen Broth:

1. In a large pot, combine chicken broth and water. Bring to a simmer over medium heat.
2. Stir in soy sauce, sesame oil, minced garlic, grated ginger, salt, and pepper. Simmer for about 5 minutes to allow flavors to meld. Taste and adjust seasoning if needed.

Prepare the Ramen Noodles and Greens:

1. Cook the ramen noodles according to package instructions. Drain and rinse under cold water to stop cooking. Divide noodles among serving bowls.
2. In the same pot of boiling water used for noodles, blanch baby spinach or Chinese greens for 1-2 minutes until wilted. Drain and divide among serving bowls.

Assemble the Ramen Bowls:

1. Ladle the hot broth over the noodles and greens in each bowl.
2. Top each bowl with slices of soy sauce chicken.
3. Garnish with thinly sliced green onions, soft-boiled eggs (if using), nori strips (if using), and red chili flakes or chili oil (if using) for added heat.
4. Serve immediately and enjoy your Soy Sauce Chicken Ramen!

This recipe serves 4. Adjust quantities based on your preference and enjoy the savory and comforting flavors of Soy Sauce Chicken Ramen!

Fish Ball Noodle Soup

Ingredients:

For the Fish Balls:

- 1 lb white fish fillets (such as cod or haddock), deboned and roughly chopped
- 1 tablespoon cornstarch
- 1 egg white
- 1 tablespoon soy sauce
- 1 teaspoon sesame oil
- 1/2 teaspoon salt
- 1/4 teaspoon white pepper
- 1 tablespoon finely chopped green onion (optional)
- 1 tablespoon finely chopped cilantro (optional)

For the Soup:

- 6 cups fish or chicken broth
- 2 cups water
- 2 tablespoons soy sauce (or tamari for gluten-free)
- 1 tablespoon fish sauce
- 1 tablespoon rice vinegar
- 2 cloves garlic, minced
- 1 tablespoon grated ginger
- Salt and pepper to taste

Additional Ingredients:

- 4 packs of fresh ramen noodles (or dried, follow package instructions)
- Baby bok choy or spinach, washed and trimmed
- Thinly sliced green onions (for garnish)
- Red chili flakes or chili oil (optional, for heat)
- Lime wedges (optional, for serving)

Instructions:

Prepare the Fish Balls:

1. In a food processor, combine chopped fish fillets, cornstarch, egg white, soy sauce, sesame oil, salt, white pepper, green onion (if using), and cilantro (if using). Pulse until mixture becomes smooth and sticky.
2. Wet your hands and shape the fish mixture into small balls, about 1 inch in diameter. Place them on a plate lined with parchment paper.

3. Bring a pot of water to a boil. Carefully drop the fish balls into the boiling water and cook for about 3-4 minutes, or until they float to the surface and are cooked through. Remove with a slotted spoon and set aside.

Make the Soup:

1. In a large pot, combine fish or chicken broth and water. Bring to a simmer over medium heat.
2. Stir in soy sauce, fish sauce, rice vinegar, minced garlic, grated ginger, salt, and pepper. Simmer for about 5 minutes to allow flavors to meld. Taste and adjust seasoning if needed.

Prepare the Noodles and Greens:

1. Cook the ramen noodles according to package instructions. Drain and rinse under cold water to stop cooking. Divide noodles among serving bowls.
2. In the same pot of boiling water used for noodles, blanch baby bok choy or spinach for 1-2 minutes until tender-crisp. Drain and divide among serving bowls.

Assemble the Fish Ball Noodle Soup:

1. Ladle the hot broth over the noodles and greens in each bowl.
2. Add fish balls to each bowl.
3. Garnish with thinly sliced green onions and red chili flakes or chili oil (if using).
4. Serve immediately with lime wedges on the side, if desired.

Enjoy your homemade Fish Ball Noodle Soup, a comforting and satisfying dish perfect for any time of the year! Adjust the heat level and ingredients to suit your taste preferences.

Chili Oil Ramen

Ingredients:

For the Chili Oil:

- 1/2 cup vegetable oil
- 3 tablespoons dried chili flakes (adjust to taste)
- 1 tablespoon sesame seeds
- 2 cloves garlic, minced
- 1 teaspoon Sichuan peppercorns (optional, for a numbing sensation)
- 1 teaspoon ginger, grated
- 1 green onion, finely chopped
- 1 star anise (optional)
- 1 cinnamon stick (optional)
- 1 teaspoon sugar
- Salt to taste

For the Ramen:

- 4 packs of fresh ramen noodles (or dried, follow package instructions)
- 6 cups chicken or vegetable broth
- 2 cups water
- 2 tablespoons soy sauce (or tamari for gluten-free)
- 1 tablespoon sesame oil
- 2 cloves garlic, minced
- 1 tablespoon grated ginger
- Salt and pepper to taste

Additional Ingredients:

- Thinly sliced green onions (for garnish)
- Soft-boiled eggs (optional, for topping)
- Nori (seaweed sheets), cut into strips (optional, for garnish)
- Sliced bamboo shoots or mushrooms (optional)

Instructions:

Prepare the Chili Oil:

1. Heat vegetable oil in a small saucepan over medium heat until hot but not smoking.
2. Add dried chili flakes, sesame seeds, minced garlic, Sichuan peppercorns (if using), grated ginger, finely chopped green onion, star anise (if using), and cinnamon stick (if using). Cook, stirring constantly, for about 2-3 minutes until fragrant.

3. Remove from heat and stir in sugar and salt to taste. Let the chili oil cool completely. Strain the oil through a fine mesh sieve into a heatproof container, discarding the solids. Set the chili oil aside.

Make the Ramen:

1. In a large pot, combine chicken or vegetable broth and water. Bring to a simmer over medium heat.
2. Stir in soy sauce, sesame oil, minced garlic, grated ginger, salt, and pepper. Simmer for about 5 minutes to allow flavors to meld. Taste and adjust seasoning if needed.
3. Cook the ramen noodles according to package instructions. Drain and rinse under cold water to stop cooking. Divide noodles among serving bowls.
4. Ladle the hot broth over the noodles in each bowl.
5. Drizzle each bowl with 1-2 tablespoons of chili oil (adjust amount to your spice preference).
6. If using, add optional toppings such as thinly sliced green onions, soft-boiled eggs, nori strips, sliced bamboo shoots, or mushrooms.
7. Serve immediately and enjoy your spicy and aromatic Chili Oil Ramen!

This recipe serves 4. Adjust quantities based on your preference and enjoy the bold flavors of homemade Chili Oil Ramen!

Braised Beef Shank Ramen

Ingredients:

For the Braised Beef Shank:

- 2 lbs beef shank, bone-in
- Salt and pepper to taste
- 2 tablespoons vegetable oil
- 1 onion, chopped
- 2 carrots, chopped
- 2 celery stalks, chopped
- 4 cloves garlic, minced
- 1 tablespoon grated ginger
- 1/2 cup soy sauce
- 1/4 cup mirin (Japanese sweet rice wine) or dry sherry
- 6 cups beef broth
- 2 cups water
- 1 tablespoon sugar
- 2 whole star anise (optional)
- 1 cinnamon stick (optional)
- 2 bay leaves
- Salt and pepper to taste

For the Ramen:

- 4 packs of fresh ramen noodles (or dried, follow package instructions)
- Baby bok choy or spinach, washed and trimmed
- Thinly sliced green onions (for garnish)
- Soft-boiled eggs (optional, for topping)
- Nori (seaweed sheets), cut into strips (optional, for garnish)
- Red chili flakes or chili oil (optional, for heat)

Instructions:

Prepare the Braised Beef Shank:

1. Season the beef shank generously with salt and pepper.
2. Heat vegetable oil in a large pot or Dutch oven over medium-high heat. Add the beef shank and sear until browned on all sides, about 5-7 minutes. Remove beef shank from the pot and set aside.
3. In the same pot, add chopped onion, carrots, and celery. Cook until vegetables are softened, about 5 minutes.
4. Add minced garlic and grated ginger to the pot. Cook for 1-2 minutes until aromatic.

5. Return the seared beef shank to the pot. Add soy sauce, mirin (or dry sherry), beef broth, water, sugar, star anise (if using), cinnamon stick (if using), and bay leaves. Stir to combine.
6. Bring the broth to a boil, then reduce heat to low. Cover and simmer for 2.5 to 3 hours, or until the beef shank is tender and falling off the bone.
7. Remove the beef shank from the broth and let it cool slightly. Shred or slice the beef thinly against the grain. Set aside.
8. Strain the broth through a fine mesh sieve, discarding any solids. Skim off excess fat from the broth if desired. Taste and adjust seasoning with salt and pepper if needed.

Make the Ramen:

1. In the same pot, bring the strained broth back to a simmer over medium heat.
2. Stir in baby bok choy or spinach and cook until wilted, about 1-2 minutes. Remove from heat.
3. Cook the ramen noodles according to package instructions. Drain and rinse under cold water to stop cooking. Divide noodles among serving bowls.
4. Ladle the hot broth and vegetables over the noodles in each bowl.
5. Top each bowl with shredded or sliced braised beef shank.
6. Garnish with thinly sliced green onions, soft-boiled eggs (if using), nori strips (if using), and red chili flakes or chili oil (if using) for added heat.
7. Serve immediately and enjoy your Braised Beef Shank Ramen!

This recipe serves 4. Adjust quantities based on your preference and enjoy the rich and comforting flavors of Braised Beef Shank Ramen!

Egg Drop Ramen

Ingredients:

- 4 packs of fresh ramen noodles (or dried, follow package instructions)
- 6 cups chicken or vegetable broth
- 2 cups water
- 2 tablespoons soy sauce (or tamari for gluten-free)
- 1 tablespoon sesame oil
- 2 cloves garlic, minced
- 1 tablespoon grated ginger
- Salt and pepper to taste
- 4 eggs
- Thinly sliced green onions (for garnish)
- Red chili flakes or chili oil (optional, for heat)

Instructions:

1. In a large pot, combine chicken or vegetable broth and water. Bring to a simmer over medium heat.
2. Stir in soy sauce, sesame oil, minced garlic, grated ginger, salt, and pepper. Simmer for about 5 minutes to allow flavors to meld. Taste and adjust seasoning if needed.
3. While the broth is simmering, bring another pot of water to a boil. Cook the ramen noodles according to package instructions. Drain and rinse under cold water to stop cooking. Divide noodles among serving bowls.
4. In a small bowl, beat the eggs lightly with a fork or whisk.
5. Once the broth is simmering, slowly drizzle the beaten eggs into the broth while stirring gently in a circular motion. The eggs will cook and create ribbons in the broth.
6. Turn off the heat and immediately ladle the hot broth and egg ribbons over the noodles in each bowl.
7. Garnish each bowl with thinly sliced green onions and red chili flakes or chili oil (if using).
8. Serve immediately and enjoy your Egg Drop Ramen!

This recipe serves 4. Adjust quantities based on your preference and enjoy this comforting and satisfying Egg Drop Ramen with silky egg ribbons in flavorful broth!

Ginger Scallion Ramen

Ingredients:

For the Ginger Scallion Sauce:

- 1/2 cup chopped scallions (green onions), both green and white parts
- 2 tablespoons grated ginger
- 2 cloves garlic, minced
- 2 tablespoons soy sauce (or tamari for gluten-free)
- 1 tablespoon rice vinegar
- 1 tablespoon sesame oil
- 1 teaspoon sugar
- Red chili flakes or chili oil, to taste (optional)

For the Ramen:

- 4 packs of fresh ramen noodles (or dried, follow package instructions)
- 6 cups chicken or vegetable broth
- 2 cups water
- Salt and pepper to taste
- Thinly sliced green onions (for garnish)
- Soft-boiled eggs (optional, for topping)
- Nori (seaweed sheets), cut into strips (optional, for garnish)

Instructions:

Prepare the Ginger Scallion Sauce:

1. In a bowl, combine chopped scallions, grated ginger, minced garlic, soy sauce, rice vinegar, sesame oil, sugar, and red chili flakes or chili oil (if using). Mix well and set aside.

Make the Ramen:

1. In a large pot, combine chicken or vegetable broth and water. Bring to a simmer over medium heat.
2. Season with salt and pepper to taste.
3. Cook the ramen noodles according to package instructions. Drain and rinse under cold water to stop cooking. Divide noodles among serving bowls.
4. Ladle the hot broth over the noodles in each bowl.
5. Spoon a generous amount of ginger scallion sauce over each bowl of ramen.
6. If using, top each bowl with thinly sliced green onions, soft-boiled eggs, and nori strips.
7. Serve immediately and enjoy your Ginger Scallion Ramen!

This recipe serves 4. Adjust quantities based on your preference and enjoy the fresh and aromatic flavors of Ginger Scallion Ramen!

Spicy Pork and Bean Sprouts Ramen

Ingredients:

For the Spicy Pork:

- 1 lb ground pork
- 2 tablespoons vegetable oil
- 2 cloves garlic, minced
- 1 tablespoon grated ginger
- 2 tablespoons gochujang (Korean red chili paste)
- 1 tablespoon soy sauce
- 1 tablespoon sesame oil
- 1 tablespoon sugar
- Salt and pepper to taste

For the Ramen:

- 4 packs of fresh ramen noodles (or dried, follow package instructions)
- 6 cups chicken or pork broth
- 2 cups water
- 2 tablespoons soy sauce (or tamari for gluten-free)
- 1 tablespoon sesame oil
- 2 cloves garlic, minced
- 1 tablespoon grated ginger
- Salt and pepper to taste
- 4 cups bean sprouts, washed and trimmed
- Thinly sliced green onions (for garnish)
- Soft-boiled eggs (optional, for topping)
- Nori (seaweed sheets), cut into strips (optional, for garnish)
- Red chili flakes or chili oil (optional, for extra heat)

Instructions:

Prepare the Spicy Pork:

1. Heat vegetable oil in a large skillet or wok over medium-high heat. Add minced garlic and grated ginger, sauté until fragrant.
2. Add ground pork to the skillet, breaking it up with a spoon. Cook until pork is browned and cooked through, about 5-7 minutes.
3. Stir in gochujang, soy sauce, sesame oil, sugar, salt, and pepper. Cook for another 2-3 minutes until well combined and heated through. Remove from heat and set aside.

Make the Ramen Broth:

1. In a large pot, combine chicken or pork broth and water. Bring to a simmer over medium heat.
2. Stir in soy sauce, sesame oil, minced garlic, grated ginger, salt, and pepper. Simmer for about 5 minutes to allow flavors to meld. Taste and adjust seasoning if needed.

Prepare the Ramen Noodles and Bean Sprouts:

1. Cook the ramen noodles according to package instructions. Drain and rinse under cold water to stop cooking. Divide noodles among serving bowls.
2. In the same pot of boiling water used for noodles, blanch bean sprouts for 1-2 minutes until tender-crisp. Drain and divide among serving bowls.

Assemble the Spicy Pork and Bean Sprouts Ramen:

1. Ladle the hot broth over the noodles and bean sprouts in each bowl.
2. Top each bowl with a generous portion of spicy pork.
3. Garnish with thinly sliced green onions, soft-boiled eggs (if using), nori strips (if using), and red chili flakes or chili oil (if using) for extra heat.
4. Serve immediately and enjoy your Spicy Pork and Bean Sprouts Ramen!

This recipe serves 4. Adjust quantities based on your preference and enjoy the spicy and savory flavors of this homemade ramen dish!

Chicken and Spinach Ramen

Ingredients:

For the Chicken:

- 2 boneless, skinless chicken breasts
- Salt and pepper to taste
- 1 tablespoon vegetable oil

For the Ramen:

- 4 packs of fresh ramen noodles (or dried, follow package instructions)
- 6 cups chicken broth
- 2 cups water
- 2 tablespoons soy sauce (or tamari for gluten-free)
- 1 tablespoon sesame oil
- 2 cloves garlic, minced
- 1 tablespoon grated ginger
- 4 cups fresh spinach, washed and trimmed
- Salt and pepper to taste

Additional Ingredients:

- Thinly sliced green onions (for garnish)
- Soft-boiled eggs (optional, for topping)
- Nori (seaweed sheets), cut into strips (optional, for garnish)
- Red chili flakes or chili oil (optional, for heat)

Instructions:

Prepare the Chicken:

1. Season chicken breasts with salt and pepper.
2. Heat vegetable oil in a skillet over medium-high heat. Add chicken breasts and cook until browned on both sides and cooked through, about 6-7 minutes per side. Remove from heat and let it rest for a few minutes. Slice or shred the chicken thinly.

Make the Ramen:

1. In a large pot, combine chicken broth and water. Bring to a simmer over medium heat.
2. Stir in soy sauce, sesame oil, minced garlic, grated ginger, salt, and pepper. Simmer for about 5 minutes to allow flavors to meld. Taste and adjust seasoning if needed.
3. Add fresh spinach to the pot and cook until wilted, about 1-2 minutes.
4. Cook the ramen noodles according to package instructions. Drain and rinse under cold water to stop cooking. Divide noodles among serving bowls.

Assemble the Chicken and Spinach Ramen:

1. Ladle the hot broth and spinach over the noodles in each bowl.
2. Top each bowl with sliced or shredded chicken.
3. Garnish with thinly sliced green onions, soft-boiled eggs (if using), nori strips (if using), and red chili flakes or chili oil (if using) for added heat.
4. Serve immediately and enjoy your Chicken and Spinach Ramen!

This recipe serves 4. Adjust quantities based on your preference and enjoy the comforting and nutritious flavors of Chicken and Spinach Ramen!

Fried Tofu Ramen

Ingredients:

For the Fried Tofu:

- 1 block (14-16 oz) firm tofu, drained and cut into cubes
- 2 tablespoons soy sauce
- 1 tablespoon sesame oil
- 1 tablespoon cornstarch
- Vegetable oil for frying

For the Ramen:

- 4 packs of fresh ramen noodles (or dried, follow package instructions)
- 6 cups vegetable broth
- 2 cups water
- 2 tablespoons soy sauce (or tamari for gluten-free)
- 1 tablespoon sesame oil
- 2 cloves garlic, minced
- 1 tablespoon grated ginger
- Salt and pepper to taste

Additional Ingredients:

- Thinly sliced green onions (for garnish)
- Baby bok choy or spinach, washed and trimmed
- Soft-boiled eggs (optional, for topping)
- Nori (seaweed sheets), cut into strips (optional, for garnish)
- Red chili flakes or chili oil (optional, for heat)

Instructions:

Prepare the Fried Tofu:

1. In a bowl, combine soy sauce, sesame oil, and cornstarch. Add tofu cubes and gently toss to coat.
2. Heat vegetable oil in a large skillet or frying pan over medium-high heat. Carefully add tofu cubes in a single layer (work in batches if needed). Fry until crispy and golden brown on all sides, about 4-5 minutes per side. Remove tofu from skillet and place on a paper towel-lined plate to drain excess oil.

Make the Ramen:

1. In a large pot, combine vegetable broth and water. Bring to a simmer over medium heat.

2. Stir in soy sauce, sesame oil, minced garlic, grated ginger, salt, and pepper. Simmer for about 5 minutes to allow flavors to meld. Taste and adjust seasoning if needed.
3. In the same pot of simmering broth, add baby bok choy or spinach and cook until tender-crisp, about 1-2 minutes. Remove from heat.
4. Cook the ramen noodles according to package instructions. Drain and rinse under cold water to stop cooking. Divide noodles among serving bowls.

Assemble the Fried Tofu Ramen:

1. Ladle the hot broth and vegetables over the noodles in each bowl.
2. Top each bowl with crispy fried tofu.
3. Garnish with thinly sliced green onions, soft-boiled eggs (if using), nori strips (if using), and red chili flakes or chili oil (if using) for added heat.
4. Serve immediately and enjoy your Fried Tofu Ramen!

This recipe serves 4. Adjust quantities based on your preference and enjoy the crunchy texture and savory flavors of Fried Tofu Ramen!

Sesame Peanut Ramen

Ingredients:

For the Sesame Peanut Sauce:

- 1/4 cup smooth peanut butter
- 2 tablespoons soy sauce (or tamari for gluten-free)
- 1 tablespoon sesame oil
- 1 tablespoon rice vinegar
- 1 tablespoon honey or maple syrup
- 1 teaspoon grated ginger
- 2 cloves garlic, minced
- 1/2 cup water (adjust consistency as needed)

For the Ramen:

- 4 packs of fresh ramen noodles (or dried, follow package instructions)
- 6 cups vegetable or chicken broth
- 2 cups water
- 2 tablespoons soy sauce (or tamari for gluten-free)
- 1 tablespoon sesame oil
- 2 cloves garlic, minced
- Salt and pepper to taste

Optional Garnishes:

- Thinly sliced green onions
- Bean sprouts
- Thinly sliced red bell pepper
- Crushed peanuts
- Red chili flakes or chili oil (for heat)

Instructions:

Prepare the Sesame Peanut Sauce:

1. In a small bowl, whisk together peanut butter, soy sauce, sesame oil, rice vinegar, honey or maple syrup, grated ginger, minced garlic, and water until smooth. Adjust water quantity to achieve desired sauce consistency. Set aside.

Make the Ramen:

1. In a large pot, combine vegetable or chicken broth and water. Bring to a simmer over medium heat.

2. Stir in soy sauce, sesame oil, and minced garlic. Simmer for about 5 minutes to allow flavors to meld. Taste and adjust seasoning with salt and pepper if needed.
3. Cook the ramen noodles according to package instructions. Drain and rinse under cold water to stop cooking. Divide noodles among serving bowls.

Assemble the Sesame Peanut Ramen:

1. Ladle the hot broth over the noodles in each bowl.
2. Stir the sesame peanut sauce again to ensure it's well mixed, then spoon a generous amount over the noodles and broth.
3. Garnish with thinly sliced green onions, bean sprouts, thinly sliced red bell pepper, crushed peanuts, and red chili flakes or chili oil (if using) for added heat.
4. Serve immediately and enjoy your Sesame Peanut Ramen!

This recipe serves 4. Adjust quantities based on your preference and enjoy the creamy, nutty flavors of Sesame Peanut Ramen!

Double Cooked Pork Ramen

Ingredients:

For the Double Cooked Pork:

- 1 lb pork belly, thinly sliced
- 2 tablespoons vegetable oil
- 2 tablespoons soy sauce
- 1 tablespoon Shaoxing wine (or dry sherry)
- 1 tablespoon sugar
- 2 cloves garlic, minced
- 1 tablespoon grated ginger
- 2 green onions, sliced diagonally

For the Ramen:

- 4 packs of fresh ramen noodles (or dried, follow package instructions)
- 6 cups pork or chicken broth
- 2 cups water
- 2 tablespoons soy sauce (or tamari for gluten-free)
- 1 tablespoon sesame oil
- 2 cloves garlic, minced
- 1 tablespoon grated ginger
- Salt and pepper to taste

Additional Ingredients:

- Baby bok choy or spinach, washed and trimmed
- Thinly sliced green onions (for garnish)
- Soft-boiled eggs (optional, for topping)
- Nori (seaweed sheets), cut into strips (optional, for garnish)
- Red chili flakes or chili oil (optional, for heat)

Instructions:

Prepare the Double Cooked Pork:

1. Heat vegetable oil in a large skillet or wok over medium-high heat. Add pork belly slices and cook until browned and crispy on both sides, about 3-4 minutes per side. Remove from skillet and set aside.
2. In the same skillet, add minced garlic, grated ginger, and sliced green onions. Cook for 1-2 minutes until aromatic.
3. Return the pork belly slices to the skillet. Add soy sauce, Shaoxing wine (or dry sherry), and sugar. Stir-fry for another 2-3 minutes until the pork is coated in the sauce and heated through. Remove from heat and set aside.

Make the Ramen:

1. In a large pot, combine pork or chicken broth and water. Bring to a simmer over medium heat.
2. Stir in soy sauce, sesame oil, minced garlic, grated ginger, salt, and pepper. Simmer for about 5 minutes to allow flavors to meld. Taste and adjust seasoning if needed.
3. Add baby bok choy or spinach to the pot and cook until wilted, about 1-2 minutes. Remove from heat.
4. Cook the ramen noodles according to package instructions. Drain and rinse under cold water to stop cooking. Divide noodles among serving bowls.

Assemble the Double Cooked Pork Ramen:

1. Ladle the hot broth and vegetables over the noodles in each bowl.
2. Top each bowl with slices of double cooked pork.
3. Garnish with thinly sliced green onions, soft-boiled eggs (if using), nori strips (if using), and red chili flakes or chili oil (if using) for added heat.
4. Serve immediately and enjoy your Double Cooked Pork Ramen!

This recipe serves 4. Adjust quantities based on your preference and enjoy the rich and savory flavors of Double Cooked Pork Ramen!